Rob –

Cheers to the green lights ahead, and making Better Decisions Faster together. Paul

PRAISE FOR
BETTER DECISIONS FASTER

"Every day we're faced with tens of thousands of decisions that create our lives—so many that it can seem impossible to be courageous and confident in our choices and avoid being crippled by indecision. In *Better Decisions Faster*, Paul Epstein has cracked the code by using the most human of tools to simplify even the most paralyzing forks in the road. It's your ultimate guide to confidence and courage—one decision at a time."

MEL ROBBINS, *New York Times* bestselling author of *The Five-Second Rule* and *The High 5 Habit*

"In *Better Decisions Faster*, Paul Epstein hits the nail on the head. Improved decision-making is the very point of all other leadership skills in today's perpetually changing world. With his highly practical solution (the Head + Heart = Hands Equation), you won't just get better and more efficient at navigating the 35,000-plus decisions we make per day. You'll free yourself to focus on the essential choices that truly matter!"

GREG MCKEOWN, author of the *New York Times* bestsellers *Essentialism* and *Effortless*

"One of the best and fastest decisions I ever made was to attack each day with an undaunted mindset. *Better Decisions Faster* doubles down on this premise and aligns head with heart to set anyone on the right track. Buy this book!"

KARA GOLDIN, founder, Hint Water, and *Wall Street Journal* bestselling author of *Undaunted*

"I am a big believer that the worst decision is indecision. I have been making fast decisions my whole life, and I use a basic framework. What Paul Epstein lays out in *Better Decisions Faster* is a tool and guide I wish I'd had forty years ago. Your decisions are the tracks your life runs on. Get them right. Get the book."

JOE DE SENA, *New York Times* bestselling author of *Spartan Up*, founder and CEO of *Spartan*, and cofounder of Spartan Race

"Reading this gem of a book by Paul Epstein might be one of the most important decisions you'll make. It will help you make better decisions moving forward while contributing to your success and happiness."

TAL BEN-SHAHAR, *New York Times* bestselling author of *Happier*

"In *Better Decisions Faster*, Paul Epstein introduces a revolutionary solution to unlock our mindset, lead with authenticity, and drive purposeful action. He calls it the Head + Heart = Hands Equation. I call it a FastPass to positivity that will energize you for years to come. It will make us all better leaders and team members, parents and partners, students of life, and managers of self. Pick up the book. It could be one of the best and fastest decisions you've ever made."

JON GORDON, twelve-time bestselling author of *The Energy Bus* and *The Power of Positive Leadership*

"From winning Super Bowls and sales pitches to leading teams and organizations, it always comes back to the decisions we make and the actions we take. How do you know you're making the right call? And how do you accelerate the results that truly matter? The answers live in *Better Decisions Faster*. A master class on how to win one day, one decision, and one action at a time. This could be the greatest training camp of all!"

ROBERT GALLO, senior vice president of business development, National Football League

"Having made some pretty significant decisions in life, what has always been lacking is a 'go-to' manual that entire teams and organizations could align and rally around—a proven guide to make better decisions faster, together. Thanks to Paul Epstein, you're now holding the playbook."

HOWARD BEHAR, former president, Starbucks Coffee, and author of *It's Not about the Coffee* and *The Magic Cup*

"Paul Epstein has done it again. In a world where stress, anxiety, and pressures are rising by the day, we often get paralyzed and stuck at our most critical forks in the road. *Better Decisions Faster* offers an elegantly simple formula for tackling our toughest choices with ease, peace of mind, and speed. Think of it as a cheat code for confident leadership."

SCOTT O'NEIL, CEO, Merlin Entertainments; former CEO, Philadelphia 76ers and New Jersey Devils; former president, Madison Square Garden; and bestselling author of *Be Where Your Feet Are*

"Within many organizations, there is often tension between the creative and the analytical approaches for evaluating decisions. *Better Decisions Faster* provides an effective and practical framework for marrying the art and science in decision-making."

DIANE ELLIS, brand president, Chico's; former president, Brooks Brothers; and CEO, the Limited

"For many, decisions can be downright scary. Fear and risk creep in; doubt and uncertainty overwhelm. Decision anxiety can stunt our performance and rob us of our potential. Paul Epstein's masterpiece, *Better Decisions Faster*, is the perfect handbook for avoiding these traps and helping us all achieve our most sought-after goals."

JOSH LINKNER, five-time tech entrepreneur and *New York Times* bestselling author of *Disciplined Dreaming* and *Big Little Breakthroughs*

"Diluted focus leads to diluted results. Leaders struggle today because they don't know what to focus on. In *Better Decisions Faster*, Epstein has written a playbook and a winning formula to lock in on what truly matters with intention and purpose."

RORY VADEN, cofounder, Brand Builders Group; Hall of Fame keynote speaker; and *New York Times* bestselling author of *Take the Stairs*

"You can't climb the world's tallest mountains without an ultimate sense of clarity, confidence, conviction, and courage. *Better Decisions Faster* is a master class in all four, as Paul Epstein delivers a purposeful guide to climbing your most ambitious personal and professional peaks, better and *faster*. A must-read!"

ALISON LEVINE, first American Women's Everest Expedition team captain, faculty at West Point, and *New York Times* bestselling author of *On the Edge*

"Kobe Bryant once told me that *the best never get bored with the basics*. There is nothing more basic than the daily decisions we make. But it's important to remember that just because something is *basic*, it doesn't mean that it's *easy*. For many people, making important decisions is hard! But what if it doesn't have to be? What if there was a proven framework to help make the decision-making process more fluid and effective? Well, there is! In *Better Decisions Faster*, Paul Epstein makes the complex simple, removes the stress from our most critical decisions, and shows us exactly how to have confidence in the choices we make. This book is a must-have for any leader!"

ALAN STEIN JR., elite performance coach, keynote speaker, and author of *Raise Your Game*

"Timely, practical, and insightful, *Better Decisions Faster* is about changing the trajectory for you or your team to create cycles of positive change and upward spirals of success. Paul Epstein reveals an innovative multidimensional approach to interrupt our previous patterns and dramatically raise success outcomes. The breadth of stories serves to reinforce and persuade us to take the next step and to reap the rewards."

SHAWN ACHOR, *New York Times* bestselling author of *The Happiness Advantage* and *Big Potential*

"When talent wins, you win. As a leader, one of the biggest decisions we make is selecting the right talent. Imagine making those decisions better and *faster*. Thanks to Paul Epstein, you're now holding the guide to attract extraordinary talent, be an extraordinary leader, and build an extraordinary team, one decision at a time."

DEE ANN TURNER, former vice president of talent, Chick-fil-A, and bestselling author of *Bet on Talent* and *Crush Your Career*

"*Better Decisions Faster* provides practical insights in a heartfelt manner. It stands head and shoulders above the traffic of uncertainty by rerouting my thinking in a world of flux. This playbook challenged me to be intentional and take action."

SIMON BAILEY, former Disney executive, Hall of Fame speaker, and bestselling author of *Ignite the Power of Women in Your Life*

"Beyond talent and work ethic, there is an often forgotten aspect of great leadership that is no less important. Confident and timely decision-making is one of the keys to winning the mental game, and I can think of few better manuals for developing it than *Better Decisions Faster*. This book is essential for anyone looking to raise their performance to the next level."

AMBER SELKING, high-performance NFL, college football, and business consultant; founder of Selking Performance Group; and bestselling author of *Winning the Mental Game*

"Acting at the speed of professional sports but with the heart of a giant, Paul Epstein teaches all of us how to bring everything we are to every decision we make. If you have to make any decision at all, you need to make *Better Decisions Faster*."

LAURA GASSNER OTTING, bestselling author of *Limitless* and *Wonderhell*

"Making better decisions faster might be difficult, daunting, and outright uncomfortable, but it's the fastest path to growth and results. Paul has masterminded the equation to turn that discomfort into purpose that pulls you forward to achieve success, significance, and breakthrough results—no matter what."

STERLING HAWKINS, author of *Hunting Discomfort* and founder of the #NoMatterWhat movement

"What separates the greatest performers in the NBA, business, and life is the ability to make better decisions faster. Paul Epstein has crafted an optimized approach to pivoting our decision-making to align with who we want to become, the success we strive to achieve, and the actions needed to get there."

DAVID NURSE, NBA life optimization coach, keynote speaker, and bestselling author of *Pivot & Go*

"Whether in a boardroom or on a battlefield, success or failure often comes down to our decisions—so they shouldn't be left to chance. Thanks to Paul Epstein, we don't need to. *Better Decisions Faster* shows us how to turn the stress and anxiety in the decision-making process into confidence and courage. A masterful playbook to optimize your (and your team's) performance!"

RICH DIVINEY, retired Navy SEAL commander and bestselling author of *The Attributes*

www.amplifypublishinggroup.com

For more information, please contact:
Amplify Publishing, an imprint of Amplify Publishing Group
620 Herndon Parkway, Suite 220
Herndon, VA 20170
info@amplifypublishing.com

Library of Congress Control Number: 2022923724

CPSIA Code: PRV0523A

ISBN-13: 978-1-63755-573-6

Printed in the United States

To the brightest green lights in my life:
Mayra, PJ, Mom, and Dad (RIP).
You are my WHY,
now and forever.

BETTER DECISIONS
FASTER

UNSHAKABLE **CONFIDENCE**
WHEN YOU NEED IT MOST

PAUL EPSTEIN

an imprint of Amplify Publishing Group

CONTENTS

FOREWORD

AS AN EXECUTIVE COACH for more than forty years, I have worked with some of the most ambitious, confident, and accomplished people in the world—leaders who have built successful and lasting companies that continue to grow and expand in their markets.

Much of my coaching for leaders is around their behavior and the small choices they make every day to impact their teams, colleagues, companies, families, and friends. Each time they speak, they have the opportunity to add value, uplift, and encourage the best in someone— or the chance to tear down progress and innovation and take the passion from a project. These decisions define the type of leader they are and the success they have in the long run in every aspect of their lives.

Decisions are really the whole ball game. They show in real time what you value, and they drive your actions—whether beneficial or detrimental, generous or selfish, meaningful or trivial.

That's what attracted me to Paul Epstein's book: He takes a practical, holistic approach to the most significant thing we do each day—make decisions. He has hit on a fundamental truth when he says *the quality of business and the quality of life come down to two things: the decisions we make and the actions we take.*

How we win in business, achieve work-life harmony, or leave a legacy to be proud of is all about choosing to be intentional—moment by moment, one decision and action at a time, and with confidence that the results will take care of themselves when we do the right things day in and day out.

Decision-making is a fearful prospect for many people, leading to fatigue and paralysis, with stress and anxiety overwhelming us at our most critical forks in the road. All these factors, understandably so, lead to perhaps the worst possible decision of them all—indecision.

This book can be your solve. *Better Decisions Faster* is the essential guide for conquering all decisions, from the high-stakes, life-impacting ones to the momentary choices of mindset, energy, attitude, and effort. They all matter, but until now there hasn't been a framework to tackle them with consistency and discipline—so you can ultimately have an *earned* life.

If you're clear about what you prioritize and why you do what you do, you'll be amazed at how much better and faster your decisions are. You may also be surprised at the eventual outcomes you get when you don't worry or obsess about them along the way during that endless string of moments.

Paul's Head + Heart = Hands equation guides you as you get to the, well . . . the heart of this truth.

I find that my clients seek purpose over prestige. They are brilliant at being intentional with their decision-making, their mindsets have become a competitive advantage, they lead authentically, and they drive purposeful action. In other words, their head, heart, and hands are fully aligned.

The same is possible for you, and you're just pages away from getting started.

Here's the good news. You don't have to be a high-stakes investor or a serial entrepreneur to make this shift with confidence and achieve lofty goals. You don't even have to fret over knowing what your purpose is.

As you master the 3H Equation and embrace intentionality, you'll become more efficient and effective at decision-making. That's the key to living with purpose and creating lasting change that leads to more happiness, more fulfillment, and more connection to the people who mean the most to you.

The earned life is about aligning choices with daily meaning and purpose. *Better Decisions Faster* is an excellent way to get there.

Dr. Marshall Goldsmith,
Thinkers50 #1 executive coach
and *New York Times* bestselling author
of *The Earned Life, Triggers,* and
What Got You Here Won't Get You There

PREFACE

A Hero's Journey

WHO IS YOUR HERO?

For me, it's my dad, who I lost at 19.

As you may have read in my first book, *The Power of Playing Offense,* his legacy has become my purpose.

His impact lives on, brighter than ever, still teaching me lessons to this day. Fitting, since he was a teacher himself.

He taught me to believe in people.

He taught me to love life.

He taught me to work, even when I don't feel like it.

He taught me to be kind.

He taught me to be consistent.

He taught me to appreciate the small stuff.

He taught me to give, then give more.

He taught me what it means to be a dad—a journey I'm a few years into as I write these words.

That's the sunny side.

Here's the storm.

I felt like a failure as a father six months into it.

Everybody told me it was a Hallmark card.

It was instantly life changing.

It would fuel your soul.

It would add a skip to your step.

It would reignite your purpose.

None of that happened for me.

I felt lost.

Empty and hollow.

With massive tension.

The sleepless nights made me question the bigger picture of what life had become.

Wondering if the freedom of prior chapters would ever reemerge, or if this new norm was now set in stone.

The worst part: I felt like I was letting down my hero.

I wanted to follow his footsteps.

I wanted my little man, PJ, to one day think of me as his hero.

But I didn't deserve it.

That's the raw truth of it all.

It ain't a Hallmark card.

And it's not supposed to be.

I felt like a bad person. Because I knew my dad probably didn't go through this same struggle.

The reality is, I'll never know, because I never asked, and I never can.

This is the depth of emotion I felt in the spring of 2021.

Coincidentally, that is when I started to ideate what would eventually become the Head + Heart = Hands Equation—a formula for unshakable confidence when I needed it most.

Little did I know the pain of this life chapter and this book would become inextricably linked.

There was no BIGGER, *better, faster decision* I had to make in this moment than to show up and stay in the fight.

A fight to be the best dad I could, even though I felt paralyzed on the inside.

Was my head on board for the journey?

Was my heart on board for the journey?

These were the internal questions I asked myself.

In real time, I applied the Head + Heart = Hands Equation in the most stressful and anxious months of my life to date.

The result?

You'll know by the end of the read.

Just know this: the Head + Heart = Hands Equation changed my life by helping me make a better decision faster, and I believe it can change yours too.

INTRODUCTION

The Only Equation
You'll Ever Need

RESEARCHERS ESTIMATE THAT ADULTS make 35,000 decisions per day.

Most of them are mundane choices: pulling left into the driveway, brushing your teeth, deciding what gas to put in the car. But those of significance that leave us questioning, *Is this the best call?* can render us paralyzed with decision fatigue, overwhelm, or even worse—indecision.

What if there were a three-step process for making better decisions *faster* in business, parenting, leadership, relationships, career, health, and other crucial parts of our lives that was as simple and efficient as going through a traffic light?

A proven path toward clarity and unshakable confidence at every fork in the road.

A litmus test for authenticity, where you know it aligns with your truth.

A consistent and repeatable guide to action, often within seconds.

This solution not only exists—you're holding the playbook. It's as simple as three Hs.

Allow me to introduce you . . .

To the **Head + Heart = Hands Equation**.

 + =

Head represents mindset (and logic.)

Heart represents authenticity (and emotion.)

In harmony, both are the drivers of the *better and faster* decisions you make (or that you choose not to).

Hands are the action (or inaction) that follow.

You could also think of Head + Heart = Hands as Think-Feel-Do on steroids—your FastPass to unshakable confidence when you need it most.

Better Decisions Faster and the Head + Heart = Hands Equation are designed to inspire action by removing the pain and pressure of decision-making. Gone are the days of paralysis by analysis. You will find that when you are freed to make *better, faster* choices with conviction and courage, the equation becomes the key to living on purpose rather than by default.

It operates in a simple and very familiar way.

The Traffic Light Test

Every time you pull up to a traffic signal, you know *exactly* what to do. It's an extremely efficient and effective method for making better decisions faster.

Now imagine a world where that same red—yellow—green signal guides your life. I call it the Traffic Light Test. By the time you're finished reading this book, this test will be personalized for you to navigate the following types of consequential decisions with ease, peace of mind, and speed.

In sports, we have MVPs (most valuable players). Consider these your MVDs—most valuable decisions. *Better Decisions Faster* will help you navigate the MVDs of life, including:

- Strategy: A or B?
- Job: stay or go?
- Deal: do it or don't?
- Team: hire or fire?
- Financial: invest or pass?
- Time: spend on X or Y?
- Relationship: in or out?

The key to the test is two checkpoints: Head and Heart.

Do I *think* it's a good idea?
Do I *feel* it's a good idea?
Both on board: green light.
One on board: yellow light.
Neither on board: red light.
Green, we take action; red is no action.

It's that simple; it gets us to the finish line, and it's proven.

You might be wondering, *What about the yellow?* The reality is, yellow is where the trickier calls lie, and we have many of them. What do we do when either the head *or* heart isn't on board? We'll spend quality time on how to steer this middle-ground—all in the spirit of making better decisions faster.

The best part: You won't go at it alone. You'll soon be invited to join a like-minded and like-hearted community that rallies around green lights and a simple mantra: WIN MONDAY.

Win the day. Win the decision. Win the action. That's a winning life. Here's how we get there.

What to Expect

This book provides all the detail, context, and evidence needed to implement and apply the Head + Heart = Hands Equation as a 365 formula to make better decisions faster.

- *Chapter 1* serves as a master class on each H (Head, Heart, Hands) and welcomes you into the Win Monday Community.
- *Chapter 2* teaches personal and professional applications of the equation through green-, yellow-, and red-light scenarios that you'll use to make better decisions faster.
- *Chapter 3* tees up your road map to success as you build a green-light lifestyle.

From there, we enter the deeper stories and meat of the book, highlighted by dozens of Decision Drills designed to strengthen and master your ability to make better decisions faster (BDF).

For true mastery, we must learn from the best of the best, which is why this is not solely my story to tell.

You'll be introduced to dozens of amazing people whom I consider some of the best and most confident decision-makers (and action-takers) I know. These stellar individuals range from CEOs, Olympians, and *Shark Tank* entrepreneurs to world-record holders, bestselling authors, and Ivy League professors to Navy SEALs, nonprofit leaders, and Netflix stars—many of whom have been guests on my *Win Monday* podcast (formerly called *Playmakers*). You'll soon interact with them all—as friends, supporters, and fellow members of our Win Monday Community.

This playbook is by the people and for the people—as we each hold a seat at the BDF table.

The common denominator across all of us? We believe in a world of green lights and relentlessly pursuing more of them—head fully engaged, heart fully ignited. We understand the messy middle of yellow and know how to maneuver through it—not perfectly, but with intention and ownership. We are also determined to STOP running reds.

Better Decisions Faster will help you do it all.

- It will help you become a better leader (and team member).
- It will help you become a better parent (and partner).
- It will help you become a better student (of life).
- It will help you become a better manager (of self).

Does your head *believe* this is a journey worth taking?
Does your heart *feel* this is a journey worth taking?
If so, that's a BDF.

Green light to dive in!

LIFE IS A DECISION AND ACTION GAME

Mastering the Head + Heart = Hands Equation

The quality of business and the quality of life comes down to two things: the decisions we make and the actions we take.
—Paul Epstein

I SHARED THESE WORDS at the Purpose Summit in 2022 at Notre Dame Stadium. In a room of 500-plus leaders of leaders and purpose-driven CEOs, heads nodded, eyes lit up, and notepads went crazy.

Why?

Because they realized how simple and true this statement was when reflecting back on their lifetime of choices (for better or worse) in careers, relationships, priorities, and beyond.

Take a pause in this moment.

Ask yourself . . .

- **Is your life largely a by-product of the decisions and actions you've made?**
- **Do you anticipate the same is true for your future?**

If yes to both, this book will help tremendously.

Better Decisions Faster isn't about theory or fluff. It's practical. It's accessible. It's actionable. It's designed for real-life decisions in real-life situations.

So let's start with an MVD you're currently facing.

YOUR MOST VALUABLE DECISION

What is a significant decision you're stuck or challenged with right now?

Do not continue reading until you fill out your MVD.

MVD _____

Here is my big, bold commitment to you:

By the end of this book, you will attach a green, yellow, or red light to this MVD and know exactly what to do with this decision.

That, my friend, is worth the value of admission all by itself.

Back to the Purpose Summit.

The same promise I made from the stage is the promise I'll make to you.

I can't promise an easy life. But I can promise a *simpler* life, driven by a process to make better decisions faster.

This simplicity, predictability, and tempo is the power of the Head + Heart = Hands Equation.

It trumps the stress, anxiety, and mind-numbing process of getting stuck in the weeds of every single decision as we try to navigate our day more efficiently and effectively, better and faster, in a world that's only getting more chaotic and complex.

To help you overcome the rat race we're all in, expect that this newly found equation will provide the fuel to thrive rather than just survive.

Momentum will soon build. Habits will quickly form.

One day, decision, and action at a time.

Before you realize it, you'll know exactly where to head and why you're going.

You'll do it with speed, winning time back and multiplying your capacity.

All through a simple equation and process.

But before we dive into the deep end, let's level set.

Rather than come into this read thinking your world will transform overnight, let's start simple in order to guarantee success, progress, and daily wins.

Trust me—the big transformation will come. In fact, we're ending this chapter with it.

For now, focus on winning the first day of the week—the one that starts everything off on the right foot or the wrong one.

That's the first thing this book delivers: a game plan to **WIN MONDAY** by making better decisions faster. Then Tuesday, and Wednesday, and we keep rolling . . .

Why Am I So Bullish on Winning Monday?

As an NFL and NBA executive for fifteen years, I saw the power of what's possible in a single day, when the lights are on AND in the unseen hours. I emerged from this decade-plus journey knowing that there are two groups of people: those who play offense and those who play defense. That line in the sand inspired a bestselling leadership playbook (*The Power of Playing Offense*) in which I shared key findings on what separates elite leaders, teams, and talent from the pack—insights I've been speaking on and obsessively studying ever since.

This research, combined with coaching and training in the trenches, served as a breeding ground that took me to the heights of human performance, professional achievement, and personal transformation.

From this work, a silver bullet has emerged.

This silver bullet is the #1 differentiator between companies and individuals who play offense versus play defense—those who are successful, fulfilled, and realize breakthrough results versus those who are stuck, burned out, and lost.

The silver-bullet separator: people who make better decisions faster.

Their decisiveness drives actions to do what others won't. In our community, we call this separation season—and the competition goes beyond others. It starts with self.

Better tomorrow than today. Better today than yesterday.

The most significant separation season . . . is Monday. It is often where our worst and slowest decisions lie.

While others recover from a weekend or ease into the week, people who make better decisions faster Win Monday and understand the urgency and importance of starting the week off with a positive mindset and plan of action, building unstoppable momentum and unshakable confidence for the week to come. Rinse, repeat.

An old boss once told me that having a half-assed Monday is like wasting more than two and a half months a year. There are about 50-plus working Mondays a year (roughly 20 working days in a month), so "mailing it in" for 50-plus days is equivalent to throwing more than two and a half working months of your calendar, production, and potential impact in the trash.

NOT HERE.

Let the rest of the world say TGIF. We say TGIM.

This spirit is what started the **Win Monday Community**—to inspire a movement around a holistic green-light lifestyle. Head, heart, and hands fully synced, optimized for confidence, and primed for impact.

Welcome to the club.

Let's explore how these wins can impact your life as they have the lives of those in our community.

Holistic Impact of the Head + Heart = Hands Equation

If there's one thing recent years have taught us, it's how blended work and life have become. Personal and professional delineation is a thing of the past.

So while yes, aligning your head, heart, and hands and making better decisions faster can absolutely be your secret weapon in business, make no mistake: the impact can be equally profound in life.

The portfolio that follows is a snapshot of what this looks like.

It represents the wide spread of holistic categories this playbook will help guide in your journey ahead. Below each area is an example of the type of decisions you can use the Head + Heart = Hands (3H) Equation for. Even if some of these may not apply to you, realize the impact it can have for those you may know. For example, maybe you're not a parent, but your best friend is. Share this equation with them.

BDF/3H in BUSINESS

- From doing the deal or not to choosing the right strategy and coach, 3H has you covered.

BDF/3H in PARENTING

- 3H is your time and behavior audit on how you show up, from the moment you walk through the door.

BDF/3H in LEADERSHIP

- 3H provides a much-needed self-assessment to answer: Am I leading or managing? Would I confidently follow myself?

BDF/3H in RELATIONSHIPS

- From spouse to ideal bosses and friends, 3H provides clarity about your inner-most circles.

BDF/3H in CAREER

- Stay the course versus pivot, employee versus entrepreneur, yay or nay on MBA, 3H has your back.

BDF/3H in HEALTH

- 3H is the glue between physical, mental, emotional, and beyond.

BDF/3H in FINANCE

- 3H guides your goals and vision as you navigate current and future life chapters.

BDF/3H in PERSONAL DEVELOPMENT

- Maybe you're crushing it, or maybe you need to reinvent yourself. 3H assures you can do both.

BDF/3H in TEAM

- 3H identifies the keepers and informs how you can attract like-minded and like-hearted talent.

BDF/3H in BEHAVIOR

- Across all hats of life, are your hands in alignment with your head and heart? 3H is the test.

BDF/3H in TIME

- 3H gives you clarity on where to spend time and what to prioritize, fully aware of the trade-offs.

The portfolio could go on, but this paints a picture of what's possible when we apply the holistic framework in the areas of life we want to focus on, emphasize, and improve from current state to a more optimal future state, where we Win Monday and make better decisions faster by aligning our head, heart, and hands.

Knowing what's at stake with the decisions in the BDF/3H portfolio, the next natural question is . . .

How do I know if I'm making the best possible decision? And taking the best possible action?

Ah.

This is the power of the equation. It bridges the gap to go from not just any decision but the best decision, with confidence in the process, to make the best call and ultimately take the best action . . . faster.

A Deeper Dive on the Equation

When utilized correctly, decisions are sourced from our head and heart. Actions are driven by our hands.

Just look at the equation again:

 +  =

This is the synergy our best selves always seek, even if we haven't known it. Now that you're reading this book, you know it.

If we truly believe the quality of business and life are driven by the decisions we make and the actions we take, then we need a consistent process to guide us through these otherwise complicated, tense, and fear-inducing forks in the road.

The Head + Heart = Hands Equation is tailor-made for these better decisions faster scenarios.

Let's unpack the three Hs to understand the unique role each has in the decision and action game.

 **Head**

Head is our mindset.

It's also our awareness driver.

In the better decisions faster process, our head is the first signal that calls out whether it's a significant enough decision (an MVD) worth processing through the equation, or if it falls in the larger pool of 35,000 daily decisions that we should intentionally leave on autopilot. No equation required—or wanted. Do you really want to ask your head and heart what type of bread to buy? I thought not.

So what is deemed a significant decision?

My simplest response would be, is it important and valuable to you? Either the specific decision you're facing or the category of life it falls in.

As an example, should I stay in this relationship with my partner, boss, or company? Most would say that's a pretty significant decision, so you should absolutely use the equation.

Maybe the decision itself may not seem so obviously important, but it has implications for an area of life that is significant to you at this time.

For example, you might have recently committed to a healthier lifestyle. In that case, using 3H for a DoorDash order might not be such a crazy idea! Maybe you're saving for your kid's tuition. The equation can help you decide which smaller expenses make sense and which don't. The same applies for business. Marketing decisions around a company launch versus year 20 are dramatically different.

The general rule of thumb is this: If the decision is important in any way, default to using the equation.

On to the tactics . . .

The anchor question when checking in with your head as a part of 3H is: **Do I think it's a good idea?**

Your head check should provide you with a higher sense of clarity. As time passes, through repetition and practice, the decisions you process through the equation will form muscle memory and eventually habits. Better decisions faster leads to better and faster habits.

Your head should also provide clarity that this is the best call in the moment, based on the information you have available. This is your logic check-in, which can be extremely valuable if you're not hardwired for logic. Like me, you may be more of an emotion or gut feel kind of person. We *especially* need this head check as a balance to our natural state.

Over time, clarity will breed **confidence**.

Confidence will drive conviction.

Conviction inspires courage.

These are the 4 Cs of Better Decisions Faster.

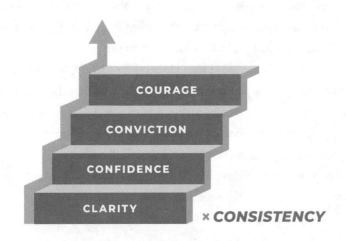

THE 4C MULTIPLIER EFFECT

Consistency is the multiplier effect of it all.

At the end of this chapter, we'll put your C's to the test where you'll have access to your very own **Confidence Quiz**—as confidence is the ante to play for better decisions faster.

On to the heart.

 **Heart**

We now shift from *think* to *feel*. Your heart is your authenticity test. The anchor question when checking in with your heart as a part of 3H is: **Do I feel it's a good idea?**

Inside your heart, like mine, there is a truth—a no-BS zone. And this is the no-BS test. You know what it is. It's a matter of whether you accept it, live it, breathe it, and own it.

In a world that loses authenticity by the day, this is our equilibrium to not succumb to the pressures, expectations, or circumstances of the outside environment and other people's terms. This is about operating on YOUR terms. Agency fully intact.

The heart is straightforward. It's either authentically you, or it's not. Whereas the head gets a little trickier with mental blocks and hurdles, the challenge of the heart is staying disciplined to your genuine truth. Consistently doing this is not easy, but it is simple—and simple can be hard.

Speaking personally, I can feel when my heart is on board that I'm on track to make a *better* decision. But it's not just me.

The equation will require you to listen to your heart as well. It's not head OR heart—it's head PLUS heart.

That's the beauty of 3H. In order to work, you must be authentic to yourself. Otherwise, you're lying to your heart, you lose your identity, and the equation falls apart.

 **Hands**

For those who step into their authenticity, we're ready for action. From *think* to *feel* to *do*. The goal is to have intention with all actions. You don't just *do* blindly. You know *why* you do it. With purpose, on purpose. This becomes the by-product of going through the organic process of the equation.

Assume you've decided this is a decision worth using the equation for . . .

Step One: Head Check-In

- Do I *think* it's a good idea?
- If yes, head is on board, proceed. Clarity wins, and confidence begins to brew.

Step Two: Heart Check-In

- Do I *feel* it's a good idea?
- If yes, heart is on board, then confidently proceed. Authenticity is dialed in. You own the decision. You trust the process.

Step Three: Hands, Make a Call

- If head and heart are on board, *confidently take action.*
- If one is not on board, solve for the gap efficiently or don't take action.
- If neither is on board, pull the fastest U-turn you've ever made—no action.

Ladies and gentlemen, this concludes the master class on applying the Head + Heart = Hands Equation to make better decisions faster. If you were expecting a longer master class, that's the value of simplicity. It doesn't take long.

The challenge is not in understanding the equation; the challenge will come in the awareness, discipline, and commitment to consistently use it. That's where the rest of the book comes in.

Speaking of application, in chapter 2, we'll dive deeper on how to apply the equation through green, yellow, and red lights—each plays a pivotal part in making better decisions faster, especially your MVDs.

Before we fully immerse ourselves in what we'll refer to as the Traffic Light Test, let's talk about the ultimate payout of the Head + Heart = Hands Equation. I told you the transformation was coming.

Begin with the End in Mind

So why go through this? Why introduce the 3H Equation to your life? Why change?

After all, you could just stay the course.

My gut tells me it's because you seek a better way—a better way to decide. A better way to act. A better way to live. A better way to work. A better way to do. A better way to be. A better way to lead. A better version of yourself. How awesome would it be if you could have it all . . . faster.

Perhaps—and this is just a hunch—perhaps you're after a more purposeful life.

The whole point of having an equation to process better and faster decisions and actions through is to live on purpose rather than by default.

The "easy button" is to stay in our lane and prioritize comfort, convenience, and "same old." The alternative is tearing through the muscle of life to prioritize purpose, courage, and growth.

In one, you will live. In the other, you will feel alive.

In one, life will just happen to you, years floating by, often feeling stuck and frustrated by a lack of progress, with your dreams all in the rearview mirror. In the other, you enter each day with clarity, curiosity, and passion, where every day counts because there is meaning. You know life is short—and that it matters.

The gap in these two lives is determined by whether you align your head, heart, and hands on a consistent and habitual basis to make better decisions faster. No better time to start than Monday.

The choice is yours.

Which brings us back to where it all started.

The quality of business and the quality of life comes down to two things: the decisions we make and the actions we take.

If a higher quality and more purposeful life is what you're after, then I believe the Head + Heart = Hands Equation is your daily solve—and could be one of the best decisions you've ever made.

Next Stop

In order to make better decisions faster, confidence will have to be sky high.

Let's dive into your **free Confidence Quiz** now.

By the end of the quiz (less than five minutes), you will:

- Have a personalized **Confidence Score**, 1–100
- Identify potential **Confidence Gaps** that are leading to anxiety and indecision
- Unlock key **Confidence Strategies** for daily decision-making and action-taking
- Access to **Post-Quiz Resources** to elevate self-confidence and inspire confidence from others

Scan the QR code below to access your Confidence Quiz now.

THE TRAFFIC LIGHT TEST

Make Better Decisions Faster

Successful people make decisions quickly and firmly. Unsuccessful people make decisions slowly, and they change them often.
—Napoleon Hill, bestselling author of *Think and Grow Rich*

IF THE HEAD + HEART = HANDS EQUATION is the only equation you'll ever need, then maybe this will be the only (and last) test you ever need to take.

If only you were so lucky!

That said, it's super simple. And most important, this test not only helps you Win Monday and make better decisions faster; it brings the equation to life.

In chapter 1, we covered steps 1 and 2. Now it's time for the all-important step 3.

As a reminder . . .

It's time to make the call. Better—and faster.

You've checked in with your head and heart; now you need to decide what to do with your hands.

While the equation is extremely straightforward, it's also designed for familiarity. When things look and feel familiar, they're more memorable and have a higher staying power, both extremely helpful when entering any behavior or habit change. Familiar cues ease us into the first step, making us more likely to stick with it.

That's the whole point. We need repetition, consistency, and practice with the equation.

So, going forward, you'll treat it the exact same way as when you pull up to a traffic light.

When it's green, you'll go; yellow, you assess and decide. If it's red, you stop.

In Head + Heart = Hands terms . . .

- If head and heart are on board, take action—**THIS IS A GREEN LIGHT.**
- If one is not on board, solve for the gap efficiently or don't take action—**THIS IS YELLOW.**
- If neither is on board, pull the fastest U-turn you've ever made, no action—**THIS IS RED.**

While green—yellow—red will feel very familiar, we need to get better acquainted with how to embed it into the Head + Heart = Hands Equation, as this green—yellow—red signal is the application tool to make it all work. Research shows a typical traffic light cycle is 120 seconds.* As you gain practice and confidence using the Traffic Light Test, you'll find many decisions can actually be made in less than the time it takes for the light to change, proving the *fast* in better decisions *faster.*

The magnitude of the decision will certainly factor into whether fast or faster is more applicable. Regardless, by using the equation, you're getting time back, which is something we all could use more of.

Some of my biggest, best, and *faster* decisions in life have followed the 3H framework to a tee. The decision to go back to school to get my MBA (process took months), the decision to become an entrepreneur (about six months), the decision to take a Jerry Maguire–like leap of faith from sports (nearly a year). In reflecting back, all were green lights, head and heart fully on board (providing clarity, **confidence,** conviction, and courage)—to make the best (not always the easiest) call, and they happened *faster* than what I could have ever done without the equation.

Notice I say *faster.* Faster doesn't always mean fast (as in minutes or instant). Life-altering professional, career, or relationship decisions shouldn't be made irresponsibly or in haste. Leaving an amazing job with the San Francisco 49ers took roughly a year of plotting, planning, visioning, building relationships, researching, and finally making the call to make sure it was the best decision for me. Without this, I, like many others contemplating major changes, may have stayed paralyzed at the decision-making fork in the road for decades.

---

* Paige Fieldsted, "Red, yellow, green: The science behind traffic lights," *Daily Herald*, May 5, 2013, https://www.heraldextra.com/uncategorized/2013/may/05/red-yellow-green-the-science-behind-traffic-lights/#:~:text=Forbush%20said%20the%20typical%20light,and%20half%20to%20two%20minutes.

As my former boss Brian Lafemina at the NFL league office (now chief business officer for the LA2028 Olympics) once told me, "The easiest decision is to stay on the treadmill you're on." The ease and comfort is often what paralyzes us.

You may be stuck (or paralyzed) at a fork in the road right now.

To help you begin to process what decision to make, let's explore some professional and personal examples, then explain how you can navigate each color to make it work to your advantage.

Green Light—GO

We'll start with the lightest lift. You will 100 percent know what a green light is, what it feels like, and eventually will become so obsessed with them that you'll attack more of them. The key is to get a few green-light wins under your belt and be aware of the trends that led to them so you recognize patterns. Patterns reveal themes, and off to the races you go. You will unquestionably level up your green game as you learn what lights you up (pun intended), what makes sense to your head, and what sets your heart on fire.

Remember: A green light is when your head AND heart are on board. So, of course, you double down on the action!

Below are examples of what a green-light life can be, when your head and heart are fully in sync and ignited. It also mirrors our holistic BDF/3H portfolio from chapter 1.

A Green-Light Life

BUSINESS

- You love who you do the work with and for.
- You're clear and confident in your priorities and strategy.
- You feel purpose in your craft and passion for your product.

PARENTING

- You know who you are on your best day, so you intentionally show up this way more often.
- You model the behaviors you want your kids to grow up with.
- You have values as a family and express them fully.

LEADERSHIP

- You show up consistently as a leader, and your team knows they can always count on you.
- You know the behaviors that are most appreciated by your team because you asked them.
- You know your gaps, and you've committed to make the improvements to yourself and others.

RELATIONSHIPS

- You wholeheartedly believe this is a partner or friend for you—it feels easy and right.
- You're in it for the long haul.
- You can fully be yourself at all times with them.

CAREER

- You know this is the path *or* isn't.
- You're learning and growing along the way, seemingly daily.
- You know whether you want to work inside a company or start your own.

HEALTH

- You're treating your body well—food, exercise, the whole deal.
- Your mental health is strong—you need to be REAL with yourself on this one; support is there, if needed.
- Your emotional well-being is in order.

FINANCIAL

- You have a plan and are executing it.
- You don't feel major stress in this area.
- You know how much of a priority money is (or isn't) to you.

PERSONAL DEVELOPMENT

- You are leveling up daily.
- You put yourself in uncomfortable positions to become the best version of yourself.
- You know the content you need to consume and make the time for it.

TEAM

- You hire and fire for values.
- You invest in the whole person, not just the producer.
- You make daily deposits of time as the currency of relationships.

BEHAVIOR

- You own the good AND the bad—no victims or blame, just accountability in the mirror.
- You show up each day with intention to be your best.
- You have a vision for the legacy you wish to be remembered by—and that drives your daily behavior.

TIME

- You are hyperaware of how you spend your time, knowing your calendar reflects what's most important.
- You examine trade-offs and make the tough call to say no and cut out tasks and activities when needed.
- You make decisions faster to win time back, knowing indecision is the enemy.

You now know what a life of greens can and WILL be. The focus is to be extremely conscious of what these green lights look like. Don't just experience them organically and move on. Write them down. Keep a journal. Start a new note in your iPhone. Whatever system works for you, do it. Awareness of green lights leads to more of them. A life of more greens is priceless. Pursue them confidently and enjoy. Better and faster decisions await.

Yellow Light— Assess and Move Forward

While green (and red) are largely about awareness, yellow is where the more challenging work comes in. It's also where the biggest impact and positive changes can take form, thanks to the Head + Heart = Hands Equation and Traffic Light Test we filter it through.

Yellow is hard because it's not an instant answer of green or red, action or inaction. With yellow, you need to wrestle and work toward the solution; it can get muddy along the way.

But not to worry—3H will help you identify these yellow areas and decisions of life to heighten your influence on outcomes within the messy middle.

We're going to go through a trio of scenarios in this section, dedicating more real estate to yellow (versus green and red), because I believe you will see yourself inside these examples, and it will help you solve your own adversities and pain points.

As a refresher, yellow can exist when EITHER your head or heart is NOT on board.

Scenario 1: New Year's Resolutions (and Goals)

Tell me if this sounds familiar:

I want to lose 10 pounds because I overate during the holidays; my sweaters are feeling snug.

In this case, your head is clearly saying, "Lose 10 pounds."

But is there a deeper reason? In other words, is your heart on board?

If there is no deeper meaning, we end up in the same predicament as every other year. We're lucky for a resolution like this to see February 1. We've all been there!

But what if your heart was engaged? Perhaps there's a deeper purpose, where it's much bigger—and more significant than losing 10 pounds. Is there a lifestyle goal around health that you can connect to this weight loss?

One of my favorite thought leaders, Ed Mylett, shares a story that epitomizes this point. While chiseled on the outside, his internal health wasn't looking so hot. At only thirty years old, with a baby girl on the way, he had a heart attack. Rather than his doctor telling him he needed to get healthy, he asked Ed, "Do you want to be the man who walks her down the aisle?" Ed took the doctor's message to heart and made a lifetime commitment to a healthier lifestyle . . . fueled by his daughter's wedding day.

I'm not suggesting we need to be this extreme, but you get the point. Ed is not trying to be healthier to lose 10 pounds. He wants to make sure he can see his family grow and be a key part of their biggest moments in life. That recognition (and reason) on Ed's part allows him to confidently make a better decision faster.

If you want to truly commit to a New Year's resolution (or any goal), find something that *both* your head and heart are on board for. If there's a gap, solve it, find a new goal, or create a new reason.

Scenario 2: Career Confusion

Is your career plan fully figured out? Getting clearer by the day? Do you know exactly where you want to go and what you want to do?

If your answer to any or all of these is no, you're in the majority. No judgment. No worries. That's why we're here.

But this is that moment of truth that you need to ask yourself: What do I *really* want?

Check in with your head.

What skills, knowledge, or expertise do I have?

_____

_____

What am I curious about?

_____

_____

Then check in with your heart.

What passions do I have?

_____

_____

Where do I want to make a difference and drive impact?

_____

_____

If there are significant gaps between the above responses and your current career state, you just need to be brutally honest with yourself.

If your head thinks you're in the right spot, but your heart just isn't in it, that's a very slow professional death. Imagine the pain of continuing this path another 10, 20, 30 years. Ugh.

I have many coaching clients in this cloudy space, and I always encourage them to not take any irresponsible risks and quit tomorrow (unless they can and want to), but more important is to put a plan in place to get out of this bottomless yellow hole, which might as well be black!

Or what if your heart loves where you are, but your head says it's not sustainable, maybe financially. As an example, you work for a nonprofit. You love it while you serve 9 to 5, then go home and stress out every time a bill hits the mailbox or a check drops after a nice meal out. To this person, I would say rather than quit (because you ARE happy and feel purpose in it), what would you need to do in order to make it work? Side hustle? Cut expenses? Get a roommate?

Start from an optimistic default that you CAN make it work, then work on the solve—better and faster.

Scenario 3: A Leadership and Relationship Conundrum

Let's say you lead a team. Even if you don't, my belief is you can apply this to any relationship in life.

You head up a sales team and your top producer is crushing it. Record performance. Your career has benefited because of their contributions. One problem. They're toxic! Bad energy. Bad vibes. Cool off every room they walk in. But they're damn good at their job, so you've kept them around. Your company, boss, CEO, and shareholders all expect peak performance and results because they're looking to exit and sell the business soon, so value needs to be maximized.

Your heart says, "Get them out of here yesterday!" But you don't for all the *head reasons* mentioned above.

You know what the right thing to do is, and you don't pull the trigger.

Every time you get close, another external reason or excuse gets in the way.

Again, this could apply to any relationship in life.

You convince yourself they'll change . . . eventually. Or you set an artificial time marker in the future to either fire them, have the courageous conversation, or walk away, and that day gets pushed back . . . again.

This is a classic example of a yellow light, where your heart knows what to do and your head gets in the way. Which brings us to a VERY important point about yellow lights (especially when the heart is not on board).

A long-term yellow is just as deadly as a red.

Whether a toxic employee, the wrong partner, or the negative "friend" who drains every ounce of goodness and positivity out of you, *long-term yellows = reds.*

Toxic employees eventually hurt the people to their left and right, so your team suffers the price of you staying in yellow.

In relationships (business and personal), every day with the wrong person is a day you're not with the right person.

And "friends" like the one described are not friends. True friends lift you up; they don't tear you down.

I'm not suggesting the solve is easy, but the solve can be simple.

Your heart knows what to do.

Now unblock your head and follow through.

It's the only way to get out of eternal yellows and get back to a better life of green . . .faster.

Last stop: time to stop running reds.

Red Light—STOP

There are two tickets into red town. One is through the lingering yellow we just discussed. You're now aware it's a yellow and just need to move forward one way or the other.

The other ticket into red is equally as dangerous. It's when we're completely unaware. We're running reds and didn't even know it.

There was no check-in with the head.

No check-in with the heart.

We just hit the gas and continued to take action, blind to our head and heart, then wonder how we got to this dark place.

Tell me if this resonates with you, or with those around you.

- I'm burned out.
- I'm stuck.
- I'm tired.
- I'm in a bad relationship with a person, boss, or company.
- I'm not happy.
- I'm not fulfilled.

The scary thing is, we didn't get here overnight.

Running one red light likely doesn't result in any of these negative outcomes.

BUT running red lights for 6, 12, 24 months does.

If not you, somebody around you currently feels lost, hopeless, goalless, or lifeless. The Head + Heart = Hands Equation was created to dig us—and the most important people in our lives—out of these holes.

The next time you sense a red light and head and heart are saying STOP . . . listen to them.

Think of a time in life you stopped running a red—bet it felt pretty darn good. A weight lifted off your shoulders, like you could breathe again. It's because it was a better decision. How would you like to be able to make more of those faster and with unshakable confidence when you need it most?

Once we stop running reds, it's amazing how many of life's problems go away.

The Highs and Lows of My Traffic Light

Before the best and fastest, let me tell you about some of the *worst* and *slowest* decisions I've ever made.

- Staying in a relationship for years knowing she wasn't "the one."
- Staying at a dead-end job where I knew my values were violated and the future was bleak.
- Showing up as a results-obsessed manager to create environments where only the stars felt they mattered.
- Losing touch with quality friends because I overindexed professionally.

- Ignoring my health for years to balloon to 30 pounds overweight (not pretty).

I could keep going.

These are just a few examples from my life.

If only I had access to the Head + Heart = Hands Equation, I would have made better decisions faster. But we live and learn.

Flipping the page!

Since I started writing this book, I've used both the equation and traffic light test to manage my mindset and govern my business from deciding which projects to prioritize and getting clearer on my WHY to influencing investments and guiding people decisions; it's been an absolute game changer for my time, energy, confidence, production, and fulfillment.

Icing on the cake—it's helped transform my personal life. Green—yellow—red has come up in conversations with my better half (Mayra) to talk about (and decide) whether we want to have more kids, where to live and why, what and where to spend, relationships to pour more into, even the highly inconvenient health goals neither one of us asked for but now commit to. The whiteboard is living proof!

Paul & Mayra Health Plan

HEAD — I know it's a good idea to get healthier

+

HEART — What is my deeper reason for getting healthier?

=

HANDS — What am I willing to do to get healthier?

Head ✓

Heart <u>Reasons</u> → ⋮

Hands <u>Actions</u> → ⋮

We were in the yellow on our health and wanted to plan our way to a green.

It's not easy. But it's simple. And over time, simple makes life a whole lot easier.

The best part is . . . it's working.

These results from making better decisions faster are why I've become positively overwhelmed with the impact of the Head + Heart = Hands Equation. Countless others have been inspired to join the party, playing a major part in amplifying our Win Monday Community, which is growing faster than we ever could have imagined. My hope is by the time you read this, you see that you are part of a thriving movement—one green light, one day, one decision, one action, and one person at a time.

In chapter 3, we'll dive deeper into the table stakes, values, and promises we make to our community . . . to ensure it successfully becomes a 365 green-light life of confidently making better decisions faster.

While green is what we all strive for, many of us are currently stuck in the yellow. If this is you, the QR code below has some resources, tips, and strategies to help you navigate your yellow lights.

YOUR ROAD MAP TO UNSHAKABLE CONFIDENCE

Table Stakes, Values, and Promises for a Green-Light Lifestyle

Success is never owned. It is rented, and the rent is due every day.
—Rory Vaden, *NYT* bestselling author of *Take the Stairs* and Hall of Fame keynote speaker

TO EARN GREEN LIGHTS in the Win Monday Community, the rent is ALWAYS due.

The rent is honoring the table stakes of making better decisions faster through the Head + Heart = Hands Equation.

Why?

Because I've heard people say they believe in the equation, tell me they want more greens, vent about the yellows, profess they want a better way, and declare they're done with reds; then weeks or months later I check in . . . and nothing. No permanent change. Back to their former ways of decision overwhelm, fatigue, paralysis by analysis, and indecision. They say TGIM, but act TGIF.

The equation works, but it doesn't do the work for you.

On the other hand . . .

I've also encountered a far larger group who says all the same things and finds a way to create early momentum and unshakable confidence by Winning Monday, one better and faster decision and action at a time. Greens start small, then grow as they're exercised. Yellows, while challenging, become opportunities to navigate and persevere through. Reds still present themselves, but they're declining by the day, and you've certainly stopped running them consciously.

The gap between these two groups?

Commitment to the table stakes.

There are three of them.

All nonnegotiable. All fundamental and foundational to make better decisions faster through the Head + Heart = Hands Equation. All oxygen to a green-light lifestyle.

THE TABLE STAKES

Consider this the ante to play. Without these core stakes, we're building our business and life on quicksand. Any win will be short-lived. Any success will be fleeting.

Eventually, our true colors show.

Life has a way of sniffing out people who neglect these table stakes, while rewarding those of us that embrace them.

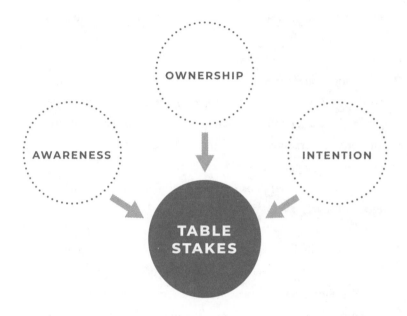

Awareness: Without it, you wouldn't even know when to apply the 3H equation or what a green light looks and feels like. There's a reason heightened awareness is the hub of emotional intelligence (EQ). Awareness of self, awareness of others, awareness of situation—all linked to the highest EQs in the world, and all are equally vital for making better decisions faster. Peak awareness not only triggers your sense of when to use the 3H equation, it elevates your mindset to know *how* to use it. Are you aware of what your head is thinking? Clearly? Confidently? Are you aware of what your heart is feeling? Not solely based on current emotions or external circumstances but rather your authentic truth? Awareness is key for it all.

Ownership: Those who thrive in our Win Monday Community take massive personal ownership. No passing the buck. No pointing fingers. We own life—at all times—no matter what. Not just when it's convenient, or when we feel like it. NO MATTER WHAT. When you operate at optimal levels of ownership, victim mentalities won't penetrate. You're unwilling to be a prisoner of your circumstances. You accept all of life's imperfections, obstacles, adversities, and setbacks, irrespective of how challenging they may be. They will not define you, or your future. You believe nothing happens *to* you; instead, it happens *for* you. Even if you can't clearly see or understand it . . . yet.

Intention: This is the spirit of activating your hands. Your intention determines how you show up—energy, attitude, behaviors, the whole deal. With intention, every day becomes an opportunity to do more, serve more, be more, and create greater impact, but it doesn't happen by accident. It doesn't happen without setting a clear intention for Monday, then the week, month, and year to come. This may sound like a lot, but these are the costs and table stakes of a high-quality life versus an average life.

Remember: the quality of business and life come down to two things—the decisions you make and the actions you take.

This is one of your first essential decisions.

Do you consider yourself a person of high awareness, ownership, and intention? Are you willing to be? *Are you committed to be?*

This last question is the most important.

Commitment to the table stakes are *nonnegotiable* to see success and results from this book and the green-light lifestyle to follow.

Make the decision RIGHT NOW.

Earmark and close the book if there is hesitation. Come back when you're committed. We'll be right here.

If you are committed, it's time to take action, as nothing in life happens without it.

The rest of this chapter is our Head + Heart = Hands road map to make better decisions faster through unshakable confidence when you need it most.

Let's keep it rolling. Gonna be one hell of a ride.

GREEN LIGHTS OF THE 3H EQUATION

Here's the beauty of the road map.

Each of the three Hs is tied to the table stakes.

Your **Head** requires peak *awareness* in the mind.

Your **Heart** inspires personal *ownership* and authenticity.

Your **Hands** demand action with *intention* and purpose.

These three table stakes will continue to emerge throughout the read.

The stakes are not solely unique to you; they're also held by the strongest members of our Win Monday Community. Beyond the stakes, we've studied and distilled their universal traits, characteristics, and attributes, then selected the most common and boiled them down to core values.

Values can heavily influence how we make decisions. When we're true to our values, we make better decisions, and they tend to happen faster, hence their importance in this book. They're also the green lights within your head, heart, and hands.

Beginning in the next chapter, you'll start to see how others in our community model these values—these green lights—at the highest levels. In the spirit of iron sharpening iron, we'll learn from them all—ranging from titans in business to heroes in the community to leaders at home to scrappy entrepreneurs to nonprofit champions to students of life.

Let's set the table for chapter 4 and beyond.

Green Lights of the Head

Knowing how significant the mind is in kicking off the equation to make better decisions faster, we must fuel it properly with green lights that align our head to our heart, so our hands can naturally follow with authentic action.

The end game: we confidently achieve our most sought-after green lights and outcomes.

To see this play out, let's experience it through the lens of a few folks (one I adore, the other takes Mondays off).

My good friend April attacks each day with a *growth* mindset, as she understands that a life of growth is a life of unlimited potential. When growth is prioritized, there is no finish line.

She is relentlessly *positive*. Every time she walks in a room, April understands that she can either warm it up with positivity or cool it down with negativity. She owns her weather system so that positive energy can repeatedly surround her.

April has cultivated her *grit* to endure any climate. There is always an easy road or a hard road. She constantly chooses the hard road, especially when she doesn't have to. Favorite motto: take the stairs.

Last, April believes *curiosity* is fuel for the mind, as it is better to be interested than interesting. When interested, unlike others who are solely focused on themselves, she appreciates people and moments.

On the other hand, Snoozy Sean struggles with these critical values. Growth is overrated. Positivity depends on the external environment. Grit is for the warriors; he considers himself a mere mortal. Curiosity is a nice-to-have. He'll express it, when convenient.

When we position the green lights of *growth*, *positivity*, *grit*, and *curiosity* as the foundation of mindset, who would you bet on?

Just like April, this is your opportunity to unlock your mindset by injecting it with the proper fuel.

When your head is healthy, better and faster decisions are primed so that positive habits and momentum can build. From clarity to confidence to conviction to courage. This is your head at its strongest green-light state.

On to the heart.

Green Lights of the Heart

Just like there is fuel for the mind, there is fuel for the heart.

Fueled by green lights of *passion*, *authenticity*, *gratitude*, and *happiness*—all cornerstones of leading from the heart.

To bring this to life, let's introduce two new folks. This time, ask yourself who you most closely resemble?

My client and bud Kyle is a man of *passion*. There is a deeper burn inside, healthily obsessed with the things that light him up, so much so he daydreams constantly, then takes action toward his dreams as if he couldn't fail.

He believes that *authenticity* wins. Kyle once said, "If you give up your terms, you give up your life." Know what you want, know who you are, and know why you do it. This is the reflection needed to genuinely live on your terms.

Kyle infuses *gratitude* into each day. He lives with a spirit of what he "gets" to do versus what he "has" to do. Because of this, life happens *for* Kyle, not *to* Kyle. He "gets" to choose gratitude.

Kyle avoids the external *happiness* trap. For many of us, we think, *I'll be happy when* . . . we get the new car, home, or raise. Then we get there, and happiness quickly expires. Kyle understands that lasting happiness starts within.

On the contrary, Sulky Susie has a drastically different lens. Passion is for the dreamers; she's just trying to survive. Authenticity? That's a crock. Been burned one too many times to be herself. Gratitude

. . . really? Who has time to journal? Besides, what's to be grateful for? Happiness. That's reserved for those who "made it." She didn't get lucky like them.

Be brutally honest. *Whose heartset is closest to yours in this moment?*

If Kyle, game on. If Sulky Susie, we've got some work to do to earn a green-light life, but you're in the right place. Here is your opportunity to lead from your heart by consistently fueling up with passion, authenticity, gratitude, and happiness.

The end game: you will find yourself and you will *feel* alive.

Last stop: Hands. Time to take action.

Green Lights of the Hands

Final twosome.

Meet Coach Erika.

Erika exemplifies the green lights of the hands on a special level. Values of **courage, service, excellence,** and **impact.**

- She constantly chooses **courage** over comfort. Erika understands that while comfort may be safe, natural, and tempting, when we play it safe, we rarely grow and often feel stagnant. The key to her courage—she divorces fear from failure.
- Erika realizes **service** is the passage to purpose. As Picasso said, "The meaning of life is to find your gift. The purpose of life is to give it away." Contribution amplifies impact. It's always bigger than her, and she knows it.
- She lives by the mantra: no standards, no **excellence.** High achievers like Erika identify that the standard is the standard. High bar, high results. She does what others won't, as there is very little traffic on that road.

- Erika leads with **impact** to be the difference maker she is destined to be. At home, at work, at school, in the community, within herself—she feels called to leave people and places better than she found them.

Then there's Victim Victor. To put it kindly, Victor has some holes. *Courage* is too brave a word. The only person he serves is himself. Excellence is unattainable. Impact is a Hallmark card.

Sorry, Victor, you ain't in the club.

Like Erika, those in the club take consistent action knowing they've made a better decision faster and thus have the propensity to personally transform because their hands are seamlessly following through with what their head and heart have already decided. All three Hs—when aligned and congruent—can be a force multiplier. A multiplier that leads to unshakable confidence.

This level of confidence is what's possible when our actions are fueled by each set of values and green lights that propel us to Win Monday and beyond.

And now a key decision. Surely you know by now there's always a choice!

Will these values be words on the wall?
Or will they be a way of life?

If you commit to living them, you'll experience the promises and payouts of our Win Monday Community.

THE 12 PROMISES

Should you uphold the values of our community, the following will serve as promises to yourself, standards to live by, and an invitation to the green-light life.

1 I WILL attack each day with a growth mindset.

2 I WILL be the light of positivity.

3 I WILL be relentless and gritty in all that I do.

4 I WILL show up curious, always learning.

5 I WILL ignite a daily passion and burn.

6 I WILL be authentic, never selling out.

7 I WILL be grateful for people and life.

8 I WILL not chase happiness; I will be happiness.

9 I WILL charge into each day tall and courageous.

10 I WILL step into service, contributing my all.

11 I WILL hold a standard of excellence, for myself and others.

12 I WILL make a difference; impact awaits.

Imagine a life where these promises become reality.

It's not only possible; it's at your fingertips right now.

These are the Win Monday promises.

In the closing pages of this book, you'll be able to download the 12 Promises so you can proudly hang them up in your home, office, or wherever you please.

Your Game Plan Forward

Buckle up.

You're minutes away from advancing past the foundational chapters of *Better Decisions Faster*.

You now understand the 3H Equation and Traffic Light Test and how both can infinitely impact your business and life—one day, decision, and action at a time.

You also know what it means to be a member of our Win Monday Community—the table stakes, values, and promises that are all critical to making this a 365 green-light lifestyle.

To this point, we've largely been absorbing information. The rest of the read is about having fun and applying it!

You'll soon engage with dozens of real-world Decision Drills, all customized for you. These drills range from personal reflection exercises (some head-focused, others heart, others hands) and action-based activities geared around identifying your greens, building your capacity to conquer your yellows, and awareness to stop running reds. With each drill that passes, clarity will form, **confidence** will rise, conviction will build, and courage will shine. By the end of these drills, you'll be a certified ninja in decision-making!

As we enhance your decision-making tool belt, you'll meet esteemed and acclaimed members of our Win Monday Community—many have been guests on our *Win Monday* podcast—to highlight how they have modeled our values and leveraged them to make better decisions faster across all areas of life. From stories of near fatality to world championship trophies to rock-bottom resurrections to inspiring a movement of millions to escaping a lifelong prison sentence, prepare to cheer, laugh, cry, and give bear hugs until the very last page.

Here's the game plan going forward:

- **Part I** (chapters 4–7) will showcase the green lights of the head (**growth, positivity, grit, curiosity**) so we can unlock our mindset
- **Part II** (chapters 8–11) will showcase the green lights of the heart (**passion, authenticity, gratitude, happiness**) so we can stay true and fulfilled
- **Part III** (chapters 12–15) will showcase the green lights of the hands (**courage, service, excellence, impact**) so we can take purposeful action

As we move into the green lights of our head, heart, and hands, there will be 12 stops along the way. Consider each chapter a green light to proceed to the next, picking up actionable strategies, tactics, and decision-making insights along the way.

Now that you can visually see the road map, ask yourself: Do I want more growth, passion, grit, curiosity, authenticity, gratitude, happiness, courage, service, excellence, and impact in my life?

Phenomenal news.

Better Decisions Faster will help you achieve them all.

Master all, and unshakable confidence becomes inevitable.

To print your personal 12-point road map, scan the QR code below. Then have some fun and mark your progress along the way.

Green light—let's go!

PART I

GREEN LIGHTS
OF THE HEAD

Unlocking Your Mindset

No one can give you discipline. No one can make you unstoppable.
Those are things you must decide for yourself. But make no mistake,
it's a decision. It's not a genetic gift. It's a mindset.
—Tom Bilyeu, cofounder of billion-dollar brand
Quest Nutrition and founder of Impact Theory

THIS QUOTE FROM ONE of my favorite thought leaders and podcasters, Tom Bilyeu, encapsulates the difference between head and heart.

Heart is simple and straightforward. It's either authentic or not. It's you or it's not. It's true or it's not. So part II of this book (on the heart) and the green lights within will be much less complex. Heart is a simple filter of authenticity; that's it.

But the mind can be a tricky beast.

At its best, your thoughts can empower success, significance, impact, legacy, daily purpose, and the ability to make better decisions . . . faster. These represent the holy grail of *what's in it for you*, should you consistently Win Monday and apply the Head + Heart = Hands Equation.

The flip side of the coin is that your mind can pollute your life with apathy, bad habits, floundering results, and a loss of hope—likely leading to worse decisions . . . slower. No equation could possibly save you with a negative or toxic mindset.

Imagine you try to use the equation and during your head check-in, just as you're asking, "Do I think this is a good idea?"

Your mind immediately jumps in and says . . .

I could never do that.

I'm not enough.

That's just not possible.

Who would ever hire me?

Who would ever want to be with me?

What if I fail?

*I'm such a f***up.*

These are the things we tell ourselves within our mind. Frankly, if we spoke to others the way we internally speak to ourselves, it would be a very cruel world.

Thankfully, our mind has another side when we unlock and conquer it.

It's a relentless battle we have to scrap and claw our way through, intentionally and with discipline. We *can* win the mind going forward, just as the mind in the past has often defeated us. And when our mind is right, the head is the engine that sets the Head + Heart = Hands Equation in motion en route to making better decisions faster.

A personal take on how I've had to overcome my own head:

- *I could never be an author. Who would care what I wrote?*
- *I could never speak in front of an arena. Who would care what I said?*
- *I'll never go back to school. What's the point?*
- *I'll never meet The One. Who would accept me for who I really am?*

At one point I said these things—and believed them all to be true. Now I emerge from the trenches of my mind to shine an empowering light on what is possible when you stop listening to your own damaging, sometimes vicious thoughts.

- *I am a bestselling author.*
- *I am a thriving keynote speaker on a mission to inspire a billion lives.*
- *I have an executive MBA degree from a top-10 program.*
- *I met and married The One, with full acceptance of each other— imperfections and all. Icing on the cake: she's a massive sports fan, and we got married on the field of Levi's Stadium. It was her idea. I swear!*

All facts, thanks to green lights and making better decisions faster. I share this with you not to boast. I share this with you to illuminate what's possible when we unlock and conquer our mindset.

You're next.

In the upcoming chapters, you will dive deep into the green lights that most strongly align with a mastery of the mind: *growth*, *positivity*, *grit*, and *curiosity*.

Live these greens and you'll experience how negative self-talk and limiting beliefs fall while self-confidence and self-worth rise. I promise you this, because I lived it, and the Head + Heart = Hands Equation has only made it stronger.

Is your mind shining green to proceed?
If so, onward.

GROWTH

There Is No Finish Line

There is no finish line. When you reach one goal, find a new one.
—Chuck Norris (all-American badass!)

WHEN I SAY THERE is no finish line, some feel overwhelmed by thoughts, paralyzed from making decisions and taking action. Others feel energized with a ruthless curiosity of tomorrow and are optimistic toward the possibilities ahead—of who they can become on their best day.

The choice is yours.

Do you stay fixed within your current state? Or do you fight to grow into a better version of yourself tomorrow? And then do it again the next day, and the next, and the next . . .

If the goal is to show up with daily action (our hands), you must begin inside your head via a growth mindset—as a limited mindset is the #1 blocker of achieving your full potential and will stall any better, faster decision from ever taking form.

The more I have studied the dynamics of a growth mindset from the likes of Carol Dweck, I am convinced the premise and theory behind a growth mindset are spot-on. You can stay on the comfortable road, or you can put in the work to cultivate a better future through better decisions with better results.

This chapter will tap into the inner workings of what it takes to show up each day with growth as a freeing and empowering engine versus a colossal weight that holds us back.

You will learn from a transformational executive coach who has helped me work through my own self-limiting beliefs, as she has for thousands of leaders. From there, you'll realize how to convert failure into success from someone who was once labeled the "face of failure" by the *New York Times* and is now known as the "face of innovation" by the New York Stock Exchange.

The common denominator: they model the green light of growth by making better decisions faster, and you're about to level up because of it.

By the end of the chapter, you will walk away with practical and actionable tactics that will give you daily opportunities to shift your mindset. Monday sets the tone for Tuesday, Tuesday snowballs into Wednesday, and away we go. Together they can transform into a life of growth and possibility.

Just like any other transformation, it all starts with a single step.

Let's dive into our first example of growth. The world calls her Sue Ann. I call her Coach.

Overcoming Your Self-Limiting Beliefs

Self-limiting beliefs are the things we think about ourselves that keep us from reaching our potential. These words swirling through our heads tell us that we're not good enough, smart enough, or strong enough. That in some fundamental way *we're not enough*. We sometimes try to convince ourselves that those thoughts are just us being humble, but the truth is far more dangerous—they keep us from clarity, confidence, conviction, and courage in our decisions; they separate authenticity from action; and they block the purposeful outcomes we seek to achieve.

Sue Ann Gonis is a true leader in the mindset space, holding senior leadership positions in Fortune 50 organizations and coaching thousands of executives across blue-chip companies, including Apple, Disney, and Google. She is committed to guiding leaders to strengthen their skills to bring out the best in others and helping people find the answers that work for them. But rather than providing answers, she believes the answers lie within each of us.

Her secret sauce? She is gifted at helping people eliminate self-limiting beliefs so they can realize greater self-awareness and accountability to make better, faster decisions that lead to a more fulfilling life.

How do I know this?

Because she did it for me.

For those who read my first book, *The Power of Playing Offense*, you may recall a coach who changed my life. After decades of collecting safe and healthy checks, I was inspired to bet on myself, taking a Jerry Maguire–like leap from a dream job in the sports industry to start my own business. That inspiration came from my coach, Sue Ann.

My belief is if you lean into the consistent practice of overcoming your self-limiting beliefs, Sue Ann can change your life, elevate your confidence, and help you make better decisions faster too.

For starters, acknowledge there is *at least* one thought that is getting in the way of who you want to become and build the life you ultimately want. We all have a self-limiting belief, a blockage in our head.

The key is, do you know what it is? Do you know what it's standing in the way of creating?

It's time for our first decision drill.

DECISION DRILL

Identify one goal in life that you've struggled to take action on achieving. It's likely a yellow light, where your head is the gap but heart is on board.

What is the goal? _____

_____

Now put some thought into what obstacle is getting in the way, likely the limiting beliefs, stress, or anxieties surrounding the goal, whether they be self-doubt, financial, or otherwise.

What are your anxieties and doubts around the goal—that is, what's causing the yellow?

Notes: _____

_____

Now what's one mindset shift or action you can take to overcome this yellow and make it a green?

Notes: _____

_____

If you identified the path to green, rock on. If you're still stuck, here's some perspective on limiting beliefs that may get you off the sidelines, as it did for me.

Early in our sessions together, Sue Ann shared two questions that helped me understand I was my own worst enemy. I was battling my mind, when no external factor or circumstance was preventing the potential I was capable of.

Those questions were:

- How is this belief serving you?
- What is this belief costing you?

Put in these terms, none of my self-limiting beliefs positively served me—and they cost me a ton. Emotionally, mentally, physically, financially. Worst of all, they were costing those around me who I care most about from not seeing me at my best—as these beliefs hindered my freedom, joy, happiness, and inner purpose. Those pills are tough to swallow—and I did for years, until, thanks to my coach, I didn't have to.

A final yet critical lens of your self-limiting beliefs is their origin and source. In this case, what is the root cause of your self-limiting beliefs? Are they even your *own* beliefs?

Often the source is external. In some cases, they are no longer in our lives. In other cases, they are outdated perspectives impressed upon us. In all scenarios, we must beware of succumbing to other people's terms.

Growth is about becoming the best version of yourself, on *your* terms.

- If you were raised by a first-generation family who said you have three options in life—doctor, lawyer, or failure. *False*!
- If a past enemy has implanted thoughts about the way you look or act or believe that have chipped away at your confidence ever since. *Process, seek support if needed, evolve, and focus on the people who appreciate the REAL you.*

- Maybe there was a teacher who said you couldn't do it, or your dream is absolutely crazy. *Wrong! How dare they try to pull you away from your passion and gifts? Rekindle that unapologetic childlike zest for life.*

Who in your life put barriers into your mind—intentionally or not—that you're still lugging around? How could you respond to those negatives today, having asked yourself Sue Ann's two critical questions, to start freeing yourself from that unnecessary weight?

This freedom is always a decision you can own.

Backable: Meet the World's Biggest ~~Failure~~ Success

To overcome failure, growth becomes nonnegotiable. Resilience is the catalyst to get up off the mat.

That's how most of us would interpret a good comeback story.

But what if the *New York Times* called you the "face of failure?" Now that's different.

Yet that's exactly what Suneel Gupta experienced when he was featured in a full-length story by the *Times* on failure, following what Suneel refers to as a cautionary tale of a career that had gone off the rails through canceled projects, missed promotions, and near-bankrupt start-ups. Icing on the cake, he was asked to be the keynote speaker *twice* at Failcon—a conference for start-up founders to learn from and prepare for failure.

Ouch.

While your circumstances may be different, perhaps failure is familiar in your past. Maybe it's still a fresh wound. I know that its mere presence could be preventing you from pursuing a deeper passion.

The story is not that you, I, or Suneel experience failure. It's the resurrection that's possible thereafter. The learning opportunity. The hunt for growth. The desire to overcome.

For Suneel, like many of us, he spent his entire career trying to craft an image of success, but now was a very public-facing poster child of defeat.

Realizing he could no longer hide behind a fake-it-till-you-make-it attitude of success, he decided to give this new identity of failure a try. He began emailing highly successful people using the *Times* article to break the ice, writing things like, "As you can see from the article below, I don't know what I'm doing. Would you be willing to grab coffee and give me some advice?"

While this was brave, the breakthrough had yet to come.

After hundreds of honest and vulnerable conversations with fascinating people, it unexpectedly led to a life-altering discovery.

People who change the world around them aren't just brilliant, they're *backable*. They have a seemingly mysterious superpower, an "it" factor, that lies at the intersection of confidence, creativity, and persuasion. And Suneel learned that this superpower can be attained by any of us.

Fast-forward several years, and Suneel is now the bestselling author of *Backable*, which is rooted in his journey from the "face of failure" in the *New York Times* to the "new face of innovation" for the New York Stock Exchange.

Suneel is also the founding CEO of RISE, which partnered with then First Lady Michelle Obama to deliver low-cost health care services to people in need, leading to Apple naming it App of the Year. Suneel later ran for US Congress and now serves on faculty at Harvard University and as an emissary for Gross National Happiness between the United States and the Kingdom of Bhutan. Not bad for the face of failure.

He's been turning the heads of some of the most influential people in our space ever since. I couldn't express it any better than renowned thought leader Simon Sinek: "There are only a few people in the world who have made a success out of failing," Sinek said. "Suneel Gupta is one of them."

What is my connection to Suneel, and why am I honored to share his story with you?

We were in a thought leaders mastermind group together, and I instantly fell in love with his aura, character, and growth mindset. At the time I had no idea of his impressive résumé or his failures. All I knew is we felt like kindred spirits, through Zoom!

When he introduced his (then) future book, *Backable*, it resonated deeply. I thought about all the moments in my life, from a high-stakes conversation with NFL commissioner Roger Goodell to asking my now father-in-law for his daughter's hand from three time zones away to years later continually asking my wife to believe and invest in my dream. All were auditions and platforms to be backable. Each a better decision that has had a ripple effect to this day.

I also admit there are many times in my life when I was not backable. And I believe that is the *bigger lesson*.

Why are we resilient, courageous, and inspired for growth at times, giving ourselves a *chance* to be backable? Yet at other times we sit on the sidelines with apathy and disinterest.

As I reflect on when I was backable versus not, it came down to a deeper purpose and reason (heart) for *why* I wanted to be backable in that moment, and often the differentiator was a person beyond myself.

Suneel shares how he sourced his backable nature and resilience from his mom, who rose from poverty overseas to become Ford Motor Company's first female engineer. I assure you Suneel thought about his mom when resurrecting his career after chapters of failure.

For me, it's my late father. My deeper purpose is to make him proud. Whenever I struggle to be resilient or I don't feel like being backable even matters, his spirit gets me back on track.

It's your turn.

DECISION DRILL

Think of the person who inspires you most. Your head and heart would do ANYTHING for them. Whether still with you, or in memory, choose that person. Now think of something you have *yet* to pursue based on a fear of failure. Jot your notes below.

Notes: _____

_____

_____

_____

_____

Look deeply at the words written and dedicate the pursuit to that person who inspires you most. By externally dedicating it, there is massive power to flip what was a yellow into an empowering green. We will often let ourselves down before we let the most important person in our life down. When you inevitably face struggle to make better, faster decisions in your journey ahead, just remember: You're not alone. They've got your back.

Don't Go At It Alone

Growth is a beautiful thing, but make no mistake: it is demanding, and it is the road less traveled—like deciding to Win Monday while others fantasize about Friday.

People don't choose challenge *consistently* unless they're committed to a life of greens, conquering yellows, and are sick and tired of wallowing in the red. Even with this mindset of growth, countless roadblocks and setbacks await. The good news is you just received a master class from two of the finest examples on how to leverage the green light of growth and unshakable confidence as decision-making fuel.

TO RECAP GROWTH:

1. **Self-limiting beliefs and head blocks are par for the course**. We now have a playbook to overcome them and transform former yellows (head gaps) into future greens. With greens, better decisions come faster.

2. **One of the best ways to flip failure into success— become backable**. If you have a head or heart gap—a disconnect between what you think or feel you want to pursue and acting on it—dedicate your reason to persevere to the most important person in your life.

Before we proceed, allow me to provide some words of caution. Right now, you are fresh off a chapter to tap into your growth mindset and become the best version of yourself. Your mind is right (head) and you feel good (heart), so you likely have the confidence to make better decisions faster and take massive action (hands).

However, you, like I, will soon reenter the hamster wheel of life. Self-limiting beliefs creep back in, failure seeps through the pores of the day, and comfort zones tempt us to reenter their safe space.

All of this is expected, which is why I encourage you to not go at it alone. You will need others to surround you in your darkest moments.

I wouldn't be where I am today without those closest to me believing in me, often when I didn't believe in myself. My wife removed fear from my vocabulary. My mom showed me the courage to fight through tragedy. My coaches encouraged me to never stop and to be relentless in my pursuit of greatness. The list goes on.

Left to our own druthers, growth becomes increasingly problematic to attain. Surround yourself with the right tribe, and growth becomes probable—and inevitable. Consider the Win Monday Community your tribe.

With this tribal mentality in mind, we step into our next core value of mindset: positivity.

For bonus content on Growth, scan the QR code to learn how to break through your comfort zone from a former Disney and Amazon executive who has made a habit out of doing just that.

POSITIVITY

Own Your Weather System

*I will not let anyone walk through my mind with
their dirty feet.* —Mahatma Gandhi

EVERY TIME YOU WALK in a room, you decide to either warm it
up with positivity or cool it off with negativity. The question is, are
you even aware of your own temperature?

Think of yourself as a weather system. A weather system consists of
your attitude and energy level. The sooner you can own your weather
system, the entire thermostat around you changes—and that can alter
the mindset, mood, and belief you have about work, life, relationships,
and beyond.

People always complain about the environment around them; it's
because they rarely stop to decide and address their own atmosphere
from within.

We are about to tackle both—our internal weather system as well as
the weather system we surround ourselves with. As an example, you

may not be able to control the weather of society as a whole, but you can control who you spend time with or the news and content you consume. It's just like the correlation of food to health: Junk in = junk out. Good in = good out. Control your company and consumption, and you'll start to gain greater influence of your disposition.

In this chapter, you will learn from a twelve-time bestselling author who has single books that have sold millions of copies, several on the subject of *positive leadership*. Then you'll tap into the mind of someone who has interviewed the who's-who of the world and always seems to find the most positive aspects of *who* they are, while the rest of the world only sees *what* they do.

I consider Jon and Eva friends who have impacted my life from the inside out. Their energy is infectious, their decisions uplifting, and their belief in self and others is unquestioned.

Let's transfer some of this positivity your way, starting by getting these vicious energy vampires out of our life.

No Energy Vampires Allowed

When you google *positive leadership*, Jon Gordon is on page one. His work has been featured on The Today Show, CNN, CNBC, Fox, and beyond. His clients range from Fortune 500s to professional and college sports teams, school districts, hospitals, and nonprofits. He's recognized as a top 50 speaker in the world, and his talks have inspired countless lives. His book count is now in the dozens, over half best-sellers, including the timeless classic *The Energy Bus*. More soon on how we can manage the bus in our life.

With this résumé, you're probably thinking, *Man! This has to be one of the most positive guys in the world!*

Jon would tell you otherwise.

He often jokes that he was raised in a Jewish Italian family—a lot of food and a lot of guilt. He shares how his dad, who was a New York City police officer, had a typical tough, sometimes negative tone—often questioning Jon's passions, dreams, and ambitions—yet years later came around to say how proud he was of Jon for following his heart and persevering through the hurdles in his head.

Jon has unequivocally stated that his default setting is negativity, in all likelihood based on the environment of his formative years. He's had to make a conscious decision to work at being positive and rewiring his brain from negativity to positivity—a mental grind he's still in.

I highlight his bio filled with awards and accolades as a signal of hope and optimism for us all. Like Jon, you are not a victim of your circumstances—rather, you will become who you choose to be, based on your mindset, attitude, and energy level—all of which are in your control. You can decide to show up positive or negative. There's always a choice.

Positivity is not a Pollyanna principle. It is a way of life, if you work at it and manage your environment accordingly.

Back to *The Energy Bus*.

What I love about this read is it is equal parts harnessing the positive energy in our life while also acknowledging and conquering the negative energy in our life. Jon refers to negative people as *energy vampires*.

Funny name, I know, but so true. We all know people in our life that literally *suck* the air and energy out of the room—draining the positivity straight out of us. The scariest part: they rarely realize they're doing it. This has been their programming for years, and we somehow find ourselves surrounded by them all day—at work, in school, social circles, maybe even at home.

Of course, the end game and better decision is to not have energy vampires in our life, but that's easier said than done. So how do we do it?

A few tips from Jon based on various scenarios:

1. **There is an energy vampire on your team or down the hall . .**

   Lead with empathy. Recognize that most people don't want to be an energy vampire. They're likely negative for a reason. So, if your head is on board with investing the effort, and your heart is authentically on board with being open to their story, then use your hands by taking the time to listen, understand, and potentially transform your *once negative* relationship.

2. **Work setting, you're a leader debating whether to keep an energy vampire on the bus . .**

   After checking in with your head and heart, if the goal is to keep them on the bus, create a positive culture where energy vampires are uncomfortable being negative. If you create a strong, positive culture that attracts positive people and energy, the energy vampires who are unwilling to change will get off the bus themselves because they don't fit in. Energy vampires don't like the light!

3. **For most other situations . .**

   Live by a simple rule: assume positive intent. Your positive energy must be greater than all the negativity around you. This is the tally required to live a consistently positive life filled with better decisions faster and Winning Mondays. More at the end of the chapter on positive intent.

All of these are great principles to live by. Ultimately, deciding how to manage energy vampires is critical to your mindset and securing a positive outlook about life each day. That said, there will rarely be a situation where you have *full control* over an energy vampire.

Just make sure *you* are not the vampire. A simple head-and-heart check-in when you feel your energy shift can be the callout you need.

Own your weather system, own your life. Know your temperature, know yourself. No vampires allowed, especially in the mirror. That is something you CAN control. Go do it. Go be it.

DECISION DRILL

It's time to make a better decision faster and manage energy vampires out of the picture!

- In your head, who first comes to mind?

    Initials to protect their identity: _____

- Does your heart also tell you they're an energy vampire?

    Yes or No: _____

- If yes, green light to activate your hands. Context matters, and you'll know what is the best action to take (of the three below) given the person and relationship.
    - Cold turkey, they're gone.
    - Have a challenging conversation about the change you'd like to see and the impact they're having on your relationship.
    - OR the change is on you, and you will beat their negativity with your positivity.

- What is the decision and action you'll commit to?

  _____

  _____

Next drill, and this one may be tough.

- Does your head tell you that you've been showing up as an energy vampire?

     Yes or No: _____ If so, with whom? _____

- Does your heart know why you've been an energy vampire?

Notes: _____

_____

- Process these responses, and if you have been sucking some blood lately (living in the red), what specific changes will you make to ensure it doesn't continue?

Notes: _____

_____

The Power of "Yes, and . . ."

Go to an improv class and you'll quickly learn the term "yes, and . . ." Why?

Because if your partner brings up an idea and you say, "No," it's dead in the water; there's nowhere to riff and go. The story is over.

This metaphor can serve us equally as well in life. You want stories to continue. You want to imagine possibilities. You want to seek and experience growth and momentum. You want to live a purposeful life. None of that is possible if we block our pathways to positive opportunities and better decisions by saying "no" instead of "yes, and . . ."

This is a lesson I learned from Eva Saha, an amazingly talented emcee, event host, and moderator—and an even better person.

Eva attended improv classes in a decorated career that started as a TV personality on the Emmy award–winning entertainment show *190 North* on ABC. She's since gone on to interview the who's who of the world, sharing stages with Magic Johnson, James Carville, Michael J. Fox, and even Bill Nye the Science Guy.

But this insight came from someone different, someone who has impacted Eva's life ever since—tennis superstar Venus Williams.

As Eva was interviewing Venus, she noticed a parallel in their perspective, a connection of head and heart. A link to their ideologies and track record of decisions. A common denominator in their success—or more importantly, their story of confidence and significance.

Eva has always been a proponent that life began to open up to her when she started to say, "Yes, and . . ." The same turned out to be true for Venus.

On our *Win Monday* podcast, Eva shared a story about her interview with Venus:

> Venus is the ultimate "yes, and . . ." person. She didn't have the Harvard degree. She took her natural gifts and never worried about her circumstances. No one expected a young African American girl from South Central LA to become one of the world's best athletes—not just one of the best female athletes but best athletes, period! She went to the tennis courts every day with her sister Serena and father, who wasn't even a tennis pro. Sometimes they

had to chain up their rackets so they wouldn't get stolen, but she went there every day and said, "Yes, and . . ." Then she was criticized for her fashion choices on the court and said, 'Yes, and . . .' This is what I'm known for, and I'm going to develop a line of sportswear. Venus then authored a book where she interviewed athletes and leaders to understand their keys to success, and I asked her what she learned from them? She responded, they all said, "Yes, and . . ."

When I asked her what her greatest accomplishment was, I was expecting her to talk about when she achieved equal pay for female tennis players as males, or the year she first won Wimbledon. She didn't. She said, one of my favorite experiences is losing a tennis match—and knowing that I haven't finished yet. I have to keep going.

From Eva's perspective, this reinforced an extremely valuable lesson:

In today's day and age, everyone likes to be happy, and I'm all for being happy and grateful. But you know what? Sad is a great emotion too. We are capable of so many emotions, and we get to experience them all. So I sat there, and I thought to myself, if Venus Williams was not mired by her experiences when she lost on the court, she just said "yes, and . . ." and kept going. Let me learn from this moment. Let me keep going. I'm not finished. If you always expect happy and perfect, your feelings will cripple you. When negative emotions arise, just say, "Yes, and . . ." then keep going.

This hit hard for me because I, like many of us, always associated positivity with thoughts like happiness, glass half full, and optimism. While all true, there is another side to the coin that Venus and Eva have shined a light on.

What if the positivity in your life can be equally sourced by how gritty and resilient you show up when things don't go right? You acknowledge and absorb it. Fully mindful, accepting the full range of emotions, say, "Yes, and . . ." then just keep going. What an amazing (and unexpected) path to making a better decision faster.

Sometimes the green light is a fight of perseverance, not a downhill run. That's why Winning Monday is so powerful. It's an uphill battle. We know it, and we never stop.

Whether it's Jon choosing not to default to cynicism or Venus always pushing on, positivity comes in many forms.

This is our playbook for how we can stay positive when inevitably there are times when everything around us won't be positive. Master this, and I'll bet on you living a positive life (of more greens than reds) regardless of circumstance.

DECISION DRILL

In your head, identify a yellow light you're struggling with.

Notes: _____

_____

In your heart, identify a yellow light you're struggling with.

Notes: _____

_____

See how the power of "yes, and . . ." may be able to help one or both. Sometimes a yellow turns into a green (or becomes a problem of the past) because of closure. Other times it's simply removed by acceptance. Both can be better, faster decisions. You acknowledge the situation, accept it for what it is, then move on by saying, "Yes, and . . ." YES, this is happening in my life. AND I choose to flip the page. That one small mindset shift allows you to not fester in the yellow. You manage the yellows; don't let the yellows manage you.

Assume Positive Intent

Quick highlights, then a closing perspective.

TO RECAP POSITIVITY:

1. **No energy vampires allowed if we want our energy bus to roll with positivity**. Remember: Vampires don't like the light! Be the light. Greens win. Reds lose. That's the BDF way.
2. **"Yes, and . . ."** While these words can be powerful in good times, they can be transformational and life-changing in bad times. "Yes, and . . ." gets you through the storm. Consider it a cocktail of resilience, positivity, and Winning Monday—a recipe to overcome your toughest yellows.

One final insight. Without it, positivity will be short-lived when the goal is for it to be enduring.

Assume positive intent.

With others—and yourself.

With others, remember that people *likely* don't get out of bed saying, "I want to be an asshole." They're negative in the moment for a reason.

Listen, show empathy, and forgive if needed. Also, just because they've been negative before doesn't mean they're bad people or are destined to be negative again. Energy vampires are not a one-shot deal. Assuming positive intent is a healthier way to live and lead, especially from the neck up.

Intent is always your decision.

Forgiveness can be even more impactful in the mirror. We've all had bad days. It doesn't make you a bad or negative person either. *YES, I was negative in that moment, AND I am moving forward to grow positively from that experience.* Assume positive intent with yourself, or who else will?

Forgiveness is a prime example of inner grit, which happens to be our next value.

For bonus content on Positivity, scan the QR code to learn how to rekindle your childlike joy and enthusiasm for life from a former Microsoft leader turned team-building titan.

GRIT

Take the Stairs

Grit is passion and perseverance for very long-term goals. Grit is having stamina. Grit is sticking with your future, day-in, day-out. Not just for the week, not just for the month, but for years. And working really hard to make that future a reality. Grit is living life like it's a marathon, not a sprint.
—Angela Duckworth, bestselling author of *Grit*

HOW OFTEN ARE YOU willing to exercise grit and take the stairs?

How many times have you taken the stairs by choice?

Do you even have a deeper reason to take the stairs?

I ask these questions, and you need to make these decisions, literally and metaphorically.

The reality is, we largely take the easy road. The elevator. The escalator. The FastPass. Cruise control. The list goes on.

As soon as Staples started to promote "the easy button," we all asked for that at work, home, school, and life.

The problem is, it doesn't exist.

The default setting to life is Level 10 difficult. Adversity is universal. Setbacks and obstacles are guaranteed. Conflict and tension a certainty. You may love the spring and summer, but winter always comes.

Winter, like Monday, is the *separation season* in which those who align their head, heart, and hands—those who make better decisions faster—create distance from the pack.

Separators are the few who are willing to step into the unknown to take courageous and imperfect action with their hands.

Separators default to a heart of scrappiness and toughness.

Separators default to a head and mindset of grit.

If you strive to be a separator, this is the chapter for you.

Buckle up as you learn the four attributes of grit from a Navy SEAL commander. Then acquire the mentality of a fighter jet from a global influencer who has persevered through a rags-to-riches story by leveraging his pain into purpose. You'll wonder how he's even alive.

The common thread: They did what others won't to *earn* a life of greens, conquer the yellows, and battle through the reds—one day, decision, and action at a time.

You're next.

When a SEAL Talks Grit, Listen

Meet Rich Diviney, a.k.a. a total badass. Rich has 20-plus years of experience as a Navy SEAL officer, where he completed more than 13 overseas deployments, including leadership of a team that created the first "Mind Gym" to help special operators train their brain to perform better, faster, longer, and optimally across high-stress environments.

Rich and I did not meet on the battlefield. We met in the boardroom as we cofacilitated leadership development workshops at American

Airlines, Shell, and the 49ers, among others. Our friendship has grown stronger through the years, and I owe Rich infinite credit for challenging me to become the grittiest and most confident version of myself.

Now a celebrated author of *The Attributes*, Rich shares his insights from his SEAL days and beyond on the 25 hidden drivers of optimal performance and what it takes to unlock them, especially when things get hard.

The 25 drivers are comprised of five core attributes, each with subattributes that bring the larger attribute to life. Grit is one of the core five.

In Rich's words, grit enables you to power through the decision to carry on and push through, sometimes only in tiny increments, no matter how difficult or miserable the challenge; however, grit is not a singular trait. Its subattributes include courage, perseverance, adaptability, and resilience.

When a SEAL commander talks grit and the recipe to get there, I listen—and figure out how to apply that lesson into my own life, as you're about to.

Let's break down Rich's ingredients:

- **Courage:** It starts by standing tallest when fear and risk are highest. Courage is both a part of Rich's game plan as well as a later chapter in *Better Decisions Faster*, where we divorce fear from failure.
- **Perseverance:** This is the enduring discipline needed to make grit stick and express it consistently over time.
- **Adaptability:** Rich believes humans are the ultimate adaptation machines, when we choose to. We'll soon connect the power of adaptation to our optimal performance.
- **Resilience:** The question isn't whether winter will come; it's will you weather the storm? Resilience is where toughness and bounceback intersect.

With these core traits in mind, I had Rich on my podcast to discuss how we can make intangibles, including grit, more tangible.

There are essentially two ways—experience and environment. Look at the experiences and environments where you have thrived or failed to thrive. You'll discover a great deal about what you're capable of achieving and persevering through.

Coming from the high-performance sports world, this sounded familiar. We strive to always replicate the peaks of our past, right?

According to Rich, wrong. This one stumped and surprised me.

How could a SEAL not believe peak performance was the end goal? They're the biggest peak performers in the world!

Again, wrong.

In Rich's words, in BUD/S (basic underwater demolition) training, there is nothing peak about lying in the ocean, freezing cold, wet sand penetrating, waves crashing on you. In this moment, the decision is purely about survival and not quitting.

Now it hit.

In sports, peak performance is required—as examples, NFL players should peak on Sunday, and a professional boxer shouldn't reach peak fitness 30 days before the fight. But that's rarely how life goes. Sure, there's a career-catapulting presentation or grand opening of your business, but those days are few and far between.

The reality is, life is largely about the marathon of the gritty grind. Peak is more about the spotlight, when we need to go there.

In the more common days—the middle of the long marathon—it's not peak performance we're after. It's optimal performance. Optimal may include those peak moments, and it may even include moments of survival (sans wet sand), but it largely includes doing the best you can right now *with the resources you have available.* That's life. That's courage. That's perseverance. That's adaptability. That's resilience.

That's Monday.

That's grit.

DECISION DRILL

Right about now you're either feeling charged up if you consider yourself to be a person of high courage, perseverance, adaptability, and resilience—or feeling not so hot if you don't.

Great news.

Another gem from Rich is that all attributes are malleable—meaning we can grow them, develop them, and master them—if we put in the work.

Rich urges us to think of each attribute as a dimmer switch. They can slide up or down at any point. Meaning if you invest the time and put it in frequent practice, your level of courage can go up. If you don't practice adaptability over the months and years, your adaptability switch goes down.

What is your self-rating for each element of grit?

Courage Rating (1–10): _____

Perseverance Rating (1–10): _____

Adaptability Rating (1–10): _____

Resilience Rating (1–10): _____

If your rating in each area is an 8 or above, you're likely leveraging this attribute to drive more greens in your life. Harness and utilize these attributes to make better decisions faster.

If your rating is a 4 or below, you may be experiencing some reds and are underutilizing this attribute.

If you're in between a 5 and 7, this is the messy middle of yellow. The first step is awareness. Now you know where you stand.

The next step is identifying one red or yellow attribute (currently rated 4-7) you'd like to improve on: courage, perseverance, adaptability, or resilience.

Which is it? _____

What is one action you can take to improve it? Pick something that would challenge you.

Notes: _____
_____

Is your head on board for the change? Is your heart on board for the change? If so, move forward with your hands. If not, find another example until you identify that gritty green light to pursue.

How to Be a Fighter Jet

Imagine this.

You escape communism at six years old with your family of five to come to the United States, with $16 to your collective names. You get here . . . and eat from dumpsters for years. Growing up around the wrong crowd, bullied around every corner, frequenting the principal's office was the least of your worries. As a teenager, you get involved in a high-speed police chase. You're the getaway driver.

Oh, one more thing. Before you escaped Armenia, you were molested as a four-year-old by two grown men.

This was the brutal, tragic, horrific (words can't do it justice) early-life story of Bedros Keuilian.

That was the rags.

This is the riches.

Bedros is CEO and founder of Fit Body Boot Camp, three times recognized by *Inc.* magazine as an Inc. 5000 company, and *Inc.* has also named him a top 500 CEO in the world. Bedros has advised multiple nine-figure businesses, been the *Wall Street Journal* bestselling author of *Man Up*, and his work has been featured in ABC, NBC, CBS, Fox, *New York Times, Huffington Post*, and other outlets.

While all his accolades are beyond impressive, take a closer look at the title of his book.

Man Up.

Think of what he's been through. If ever there was a story of pain that usually ends up hidden in the deepest, darkest corners of someone's private life, Bedros has the perfect reason (not excuse) to pull that card. But he didn't.

As Bedros said on my podcast, your pain (once healed) can become your purpose. Bedros's pain as a child, teenager, and early adult all became a part of his mission to, in his words, fix broken men—because he once was broken too—and he knows many need a lifeline yet don't have a safe space to open up and heal.

Even his motivation for starting Fit Body Boot Camp came from him being the chubby (again, his words) kid on the block. As he started to understand health and wellness, he decided to become a part of the solution and start a boot camp movement instead of wallowing in sorrow and letting his life slip away.

Another way to put this: Bedros chose to inspire everyone he serves to be a fighter jet.

What is a fighter jet?

The opposite of a crop duster.

Let's break this down as only Bedros can . . .

A **crop duster** is indecisive, loves to complain, constantly seeks out approval, and putters through life unorganized in thought and action.

Crop dusters are drifters—lacking awareness and accountability. Their lives have no passion, urgency, or intention. They live only for themselves and, for that exact reason, they never end up getting what they want (or at least not for long).

So they go back to complaining and dull their inner pain with self-destructive and damaging behavior, like heavy drinking, smoking, and emotional eating.

A **fighter jet** is an expert of self-mastery, a decider, and a leader. Fighter jets have control over their thoughts, emotions, and actions. Head, heart, and hands are fully aligned.

They are self-disciplined and know when to reach out to mentors, coaches, and trusted friends for help. They take care of their minds and bodies by exercising regularly, eating well, and reading.

Most of all, they are driven by a purpose beyond themselves, which pushes them to deliver better, faster, and greater results every day, especially Monday.

Do you want to be a fighter jet or a crop duster?

Only fighter jets enjoy the sustained fruits of green lights. Only fighter jets consistently conquer yellows. Only crop dusters habitually run reds.

I can tell you after spending time with Bedros in his corporate HQ and production studio that his entire team consists of the happiest, most inspired, and impact-driven fighter jets I've seen. It's hard to call a culture perfect, but this was damn close. The respect they not only have for Bedros but each other, their work, and their clients was special to experience.

More evidence on who Bedros is at his core: Every penny of his speaking business (which is quite healthy) is donated to his favorite charities: Toys for Tots and Shriners Hospitals for Children. As his website states, don't even think of negotiating his speaking fee!

Would you?

DECISION DRILL

In the spirit of honoring Bedros—as I've heard him say this countless times—it's time to get off your ass, do the work, and become who you're meant to be!

Coming back to the decision of the hour: *Do you consider yourself a fighter jet?*

If so, identify a recent adversity you've faced. One where grit was the medicine required to get you over the hump.

What did you do to overcome the adversity? A shift in mindset, attitude, action? A shift in head, heart, or hands?

Take notes of specifically what you did, as those are the marks of how a fighter jet flips reds and yellows into greens.

Notes: _____

_____

_____

Now be consistent and DECIDE to be a fighter jet for life.

Those who matter will be proud. Bedros will too.

Fall Down Once, Get Up Three Times

As modeled by Rich and Bedros, grit is only possible for those who take the stairs. The gritty realize that life is a battle—it is not easy (or fair)—and there are no overnight successes. We bear one hard road, one day, decision, and action at a time.

TO RECAP GRIT:

1. **A Navy SEAL commander's four-part recipe to a gritty green.** Courage, perseverance, adaptability, and a splash of resilience is always one hell of a way to overcome yellows.
2. **Fighter jets win**. Crop dusters lose. Win your future (and Monday) by having control of your decisions, thoughts, emotions, and actions—and prepare for red lights to be a problem of the past.

Appropriately, we return to the bestselling author of *Grit*, Angela Duckworth, to close out this chapter. She encourages us that if we fall down seven times, we must get up eight.

I want to reframe that: When you fall down once, get up three. Once with your head, once with your heart, once with your hands.

We will all fall in business, in relationships, in parenting, with friends, in life. Letdown and disappointment are bound to happen.

So how do we respond?

We elevate our mindset as a pillar of strength (Head). We get up off the mat—because there is a deeper and authentic reason (Heart) to get up. Then create a habit to stay up (Hands) until the next storm strikes—knowing you'll be better equipped for it.

One final value in the Head, curiosity, then we're off to the Heart.

For bonus content on Grit, scan the QR code to learn how to perform beyond your capabilities from an award-winning entrepreneur endorsed by Shark Tank's Mr. Wonderful.

CURIOSITY

Be Interested over Interesting

I have no special talent. I am only passionately curious.
—Albert Einstein

THERE ARE TWO QUESTIONS I get asked more than any others. The gap between these two and the rest of the pack is colossal.

1. *How do I find my purpose?*
2. *How do I discover my passion?*

My answer to the first is to remind the curious that finding your purpose is not a one-shot deal; it's a 365 way of life. Start by Winning Monday. That's what you find in *Better Decisions Faster*. Daily purpose at work and in life is at the fingertips of those who consistently make decisions and take action by aligning their head, heart, and hands.

My answer to the second question is simple and straightforward: lead with curiosity.

In all my work of coaching and training others to discover their passion, it often boils down to what they're curious about. Over time, with experimentation and reps, habits of a curious mindset form and passions emerge.

Icing on the cake: when curious and passionate, you won't settle for red or stay stuck in the yellow, and the thought of green will always excite you because of the possibilities and opportunities ahead.

Curiosity leads to passion, and yes, they both are great indicators of where you can find purpose in each day. So if a more purposeful life is an end game of *Better Decisions Faster*, it is far from coincidental that this chapter is on curiosity and the next is on passion.

A starting rule for curiosity: Be interested over interesting. It's a lesson I've learned through conversation, research, and interviews.

Some of my favorite interviews to date have often been with those who typically sit on the other side of the table. As interviewers themselves, they are hard wired to be *interested*.

In the Positivity chapter you met Eva Saha, interviewer extraordinaire. Now meet Joel Goldberg, voice of Major League Baseball's Kansas City Royals. In his 25 years of broadcasting, Joel has earned Emmy awards while covering World Series and Super Bowls, often interviewing megastars from sports and entertainment, from Wayne Gretzky to Will Ferrell and beyond. Not too shabby.

After a quarter century, I asked Joel what keeps him so fresh and revitalized for every conversation.

He said he feels like the luckiest guy in the world because he gets to learn something new every day. From his lens, "Perpetual education is the key to happiness and growth. The more we learn, the less the world can shake us and the more we can see the beauty in every day. When we stop taking risks, we stop learning and reaching new heights."

To use a baseball term, in every conversation, he plays small ball, looking for that one small nugget of wisdom. The daily decision to play small ball has led to big results (inspiring the name of his book), thanks to Joel's limitless curiosity.

In this chapter, you will learn from a pair of perpetually curious and confident people who have gone on to impact countless lives because of it. The first is the world's most booked keynote speaker on the topics of creativity and innovation, followed by a mind-blowing story from NFL player turned man in a van. Grab some popcorn for this one.

The common denominator: they're not worried about being the most *interesting* person in the room. On the contrary, they attack each day with an insatiable thirst to be *interested* in everything and everyone around them. Curiosity has become their fuel for the mind, leading to green lights around every corner.

Curious to meet them?

Let's do it.

The Power of Everyday Innovators

Meet a man on a mission to democratize innovation: Josh Linkner—a friend, coach, and mentor in the speaking space.

You can't be a world-class innovator without being a world-class decision-maker—or as Josh calls himself, a creative troublemaker.

He started his career as a jazz guitarist and went on to become the founder and CEO of five tech companies that sold for a combined value of over $200 million. He's also the most-booked innovation keynote speaker on the planet, a *New York Times* bestselling author, and a world-renowned expert on disruption and hypergrowth leadership.

What I love about Josh, as talented as he is as a thought leader, is his curiosity and passion to serve is second to none.

For the benefit of us all, let's begin to leverage Josh's insights on how to crack the code to become everyday innovators.

That can sound intimidating to some, especially if you don't consider yourself a highly creative person or have that "one big idea."

Not to worry. As Josh says, "Most of us think of innovation as this big topic that's out of our reach, like inventing the electric automobile or SpaceX, and we say, 'Great for Elon Musk, but I'm a normal person. How does that apply to me?'"

This dead-end inspired Josh to flip the whole concept of innovation upside down—he calls it *innovation for the rest of us*.

Perhaps you do consider yourself creative and might have that bigger, better idea but don't have the resources.

Here's a fresh perspective from a chat with Josh that may ease the tension.

If the amount of resources that you had equaled your level of creativity, the federal government would be the most creative organization on the planet and start-ups would be the least. Resources don't create innovation. Innovators do.

Innovation and curiosity are inextricably linked, so if curiosity fuels our head, let's continue to explore a few ways we can begin to use our hands and flex the muscle of curiosity toward our next greenlight idea—that may just be the better decision faster you've been envisioning.

Like any other value, when we work at it, habits form and curiosity grows.

Where can you start?

Not a trick question—you already have.

One of the core characteristics of curious people is reading. Well done. And your book selection (clearly) is impeccable. Bravo!

Believe it or not, you're in rare air. This is a painful statistic to share, but 50 percent of adults haven't read a book since they graduated college. Ugh.

Part of being interested in people, things, and places is constantly leveling up your content consumption. Our Win Monday Community devours content. You guessed it . . . on Monday mornings . . . and beyond. Today it's a book. Tomorrow it might be a podcast, YouTube video, or TED Talk. Always stay interested in learning, growth, and development because that's what curious people do. You don't have to be holed up in a study poring over books for hours. Find small moments in your day to learn something new, and your creativity will blossom.

Ready to put some of these ideas in play? In the upcoming Decision Drill, you'll learn Josh's 30-day rule of change—try something new, experience it, and move forward.

As humans, we rarely like change. We say we do, *but do we really?*

Most of us default to consistency, routine, and pattern, but then feel stuck and stunted if it continues for too long. We're also afraid (whether we admit it or not) of the work required to implement change. This holds us back from taking action on our internal decisions (that stay there) far too often.

Here's a suggested solution.

DECISION DRILL

You don't have to commit to some monumental life change in order to transform your trajectory. Interested in something? Curious about a *potential* passion that feels like a green light waiting to happen? Jot it down. No harrn, no foul.

What green light did you decide on?

Notes: _____

_____

Here's the 30-day rule:

Commit to use your hands toward this passion or curiosity for 30 days. At the end of the 30 days, determine whether you want to commit to another 30. As Josh has learned, breaking up your passions and curiosities into manageable time periods will help make life changes (and decisions) feel less monumental.

When all else fails, know that there is a power in just starting. Every decision starts somewhere. Start with imperfect, and things will get a little better with action, building confidence by the day.

Need anecdotal proof?

Let's play with this scenario.

Imagine you and another person both see an opportunity. You have more money, more smarts, and more resources overall. You take some time to start mapping out the options, determining the best path forward, and weighing the risks and rewards.

But the other person just activates their hands and decides to start. They start with what they have, and it's terrible, but each day it gets a little less terrible. By the time six months have gone by, that person with no money or resources will be ahead of you.

You can have your head and heart firing on all cylinders—it only counts if your hands bring it to life.

Just get started.

NFL Player to Man in a Van

Popcorn ready?

This is one of the most fascinating decision-making backstories you may ever hear.

Joe Hawley is a former NFL player who played eight seasons with the Atlanta Falcons and Tampa Bay Buccaneers. In 2017 he decided to walk away from pro football on his own terms, giving everything he owned to charity and setting out in a van with his dog on a cross-country trip that transformed his life.

More details, you ask . . .

Game on.

Like most former pro athletes, Joe faced some deeply intrinsic questions following the decision to leave the game he loved so much. Questions of identity arose, like, "Who am I without this thing I've spent my entire life pursuing greatness at?" The unknown answer (likely stuck in a yellow or lost in a red) is what sparked his eventual exploration of curiosity on a path to self-discovery and healing.

Following his retirement from the NFL, Joe moved out of his Tampa apartment, donated all nonessential items to charity, sold his Mercedes for a Ford cargo van, shed nearly 50 pounds on a peculiar diet that included slices of butter in his coffee, and adopted a two-year-old boxer and named her Freedom. Then the travels began. Details were chronicled in a public-facing blog that eventually caught the eye of *USA Today*.

Why do all this when he seemingly had it all?

From the conversation with Joe on my podcast, he was on a mission to find deeper meaning, purpose, and green lights—and was willing to do anything to get there. There was no finish line. From sacred plant medicine, emotional leadership training, breathwork, even Jungian psychology, he simply wanted to deepen his understanding of what the human experience was all about.

On the curiosity meter, it sounds extreme, I know. But to Joe it was his commitment to holistic wellness that led him to find true fulfillment and gratitude. Since making the decision to tap into his head, heart, and hands, he is now paying it forward by founding the Härt Collective, built for other elite-level athletes who seek deeper healing, growth, and connection.

To describe his entire journey of curiosity in a nutshell, it was a way to reprioritize his life. To dedicate his time and energy to the things that matter while also filling a physical, mental, and emotional void that 16 years of football left behind. He's now on to his next dream—and is taking it one day, decision, and action at a time.

When talking to Joe, we compared notes on our exits from sports. The closest intersection was the common thread of identity and the fear of losing it through what I call a *sunk-cost bias*.

Maybe you've been here too.

Think of how long you've worked in the field you're in. Five years? Ten? Twenty? The longer you've been on that path, the harder it is to leave it.

Why?

We all have a sunk-cost bias—meaning the years already spent will have *perceivably* been a waste of time if we leave now. The longer it's been or the more attractive the space (like sports), it may be even harder to depart, which stunts our curiosity. We determine the cost of exit is real, but is it?

I would challenge all of us to ask, *"What's the cost of not leaving?"*

If you are unhappy, unfulfilled, burned out, lacking confidence, and living in a red and yellow world, head nor heart frequently on board. What is the cost of deciding to repeat that cycle—for 5 more years or 10 or 20 or the rest of your life? That's a lot of losing Mondays. Nobody wants that.

Perhaps curiosity can color your next move, whether staying the course and recrafting some of the details or perhaps making a major change. Start with this exercise.

DECISION DRILL

A reminder—curiosity sparks passion.

No BS.

1–10, how passionate are you about your current job? _____

1–10, if you stayed where you were, how passionate would you be for the next role up the ladder? _____

Yes or no, is your head on board to continue this path? _____

Yes or no, is your heart on board to continue this path? _____

Based on the above, is your current path a green, yellow, or red?

_____

If a green, virtual bear hug from me to you!

If a yellow head gap, we can work on it together. Our Win Monday Community can help.

If a yellow heart gap, this is just as deadly as a red. You know what you need to do. Be responsible, but decide to act.

If a red, whether you've been there one year or one decade, release yourself of the sunk-cost bias. Allow your curiosity to spark your new search.

Ticktock . . .

Curiosity Killed the Cat

But it won't kill you. Rather, curiosity is an opportunity to elevate your mindset and open yourself to opportunities that are yours to choose. If your head is spinning with possibilities, great! Capture that curiosity. Ride the energy. This is the power of the mind when it is working for you. It means you are *interested* in the potential of what's ahead, while others stay stuck on being *interesting*.

TO RECAP CURIOSITY:

1. **Be an everyday innovator**. Josh shared some phenomenal tips and tactics on how to do just that so we can explore the endless possibilities of aligning our head, heart, and hands.
2. **Avoid the sunk-cost bias—at all costs**. Dwelling on the past is a fast track to living in the red, or worse, feeling hopeless and stuck in a long-term yellow.

We're now at the end of the first H—Head. Mindset is primed. Green lights are dialed in.

Growth ☑   Grit ☑

Positivity ☑   Curiosity ☑

Growth is the engine to power our head. It shows us what's possible.

Positivity is the mind state needed to enjoy the blue skies while also enduring the inevitable storms ahead.

Grit keeps us in the fight, knowing our mind (and life) can be a tricky beast.

Curiosity keeps us vibrant on a never-ending quest to become the best version of ourselves. No better time to start than Monday.

It's now time to marry it all to our authentic truth. Our heart.

But first a key part in making better decisions faster is self-awareness, as you know. There's no more critical factor than being fully aware of your WHY. What if we could get you there in less than five minutes?

Would your head be on board?

Would your heart be on board?

Feels like a green light to me, so let's flip the page and discover your WHY!

For bonus content on Curiosity, scan the QR code to learn how to unlock your superpowers from an acclaimed consultant and trainer hand-selected by Brené Brown to join forces.

HEAD TO HEART

Discover Your WHY

HOW AWESOME WOULD IT be if Simon Sinek, a pioneer of purpose and bestselling author of *Start with Why*, was your personal coach to discover your WHY?

That's exactly how the WHY journey started for Dr. Gary Sanchez. Simon coached him over the course of eight months to lock in on his WHY—it would soon become an obsession, which turned into a transformation, then eventually a decision-making vehicle for life-changing impact. But first, just like making better decisions faster, he had to confidently put it in practice.

A dentist at the time, Gary began to use his WHY to develop the messaging of his practice. This allowed him to go from just getting by to abundance, garnering a record number of new patients for the ten years that followed.

In comes the obsession.

Now seeing the power of WHY, Gary began to help other dentists and businesses discover their WHY to create powerful personal brands, marketing, and culture messaging. In this process, he coached thousands of people (at times while he was working on their teeth!) to discover their WHY and started to notice an unexpected pattern and commonality among the large—and growing—sample size. The same themes and WHYs began to come up.

Turns out there were 9 possible WHYs.

Gary felt as if he had cracked the code on the WHY process.

Thinking back to his experience with Simon, it was awesome that he got to his WHY. But it took eight months. He then thought about his process of coaching others. What started as three hours per person got down to about 15 minutes once he uncovered the 9 potential WHYs.

The obsession grew deeper.

He then thought, *How can I scale this? How can I make this accessible to the world? How quickly can I get people to their Why? Is it possible to create a WHY discovery on demand?*

In other words, how can I help the masses make better decisions faster by better knowing who they are and WHY they do what they do.

He went back to the lab, pored through the data, and out came an algorithm.

An algorithm to help people discover their WHY in under 5 minutes.

This is how the WHY Institute came to be, with a mission for one billion people to discover their WHY so they can get clear, stand out, and play bigger.

The most fulfilling part for Gary? Becoming the "start here" button for all self-awareness to advance people from "I hope" to "I know."

To date, this WHY Discovery tool has been used by over 200,000 people and counting.

It's your turn.

Scan the QR code on this page to access your WHY Discovery now.

Welcome back, and P.S. . . .

My WHY is: Contribute

Gary's is: Better Way

What's yours? _____

PART II

GREEN LIGHTS OF THE HEART

Leading with Authenticity

Wherever you go, go with all your heart.—Confucius

OUR HEAD IS NOW SET. (Mindset ☑)

What about the heartset?

Just as the mind can be a tricky beast, in different ways our heart can be equally challenging. As the last four chapters demonstrated, our mind hinders us with limiting beliefs. It plays defense; then we play small, holding ourselves back from reaching our potential—until we conquer it.

But with the heart, at its best, it always plays offense because it leads with authenticity. You know how I feel about playing offense; I wrote a book about it.

My question to you, then, is this: *Are you listening to your heart?*

When true to your heart, better, faster decisions and authentic actions await. When you bypass your heart, authenticity is a facade.

You get to decide.

Maybe you can learn a bit from my journey . . .

I know what it's like to play with heart and also what it's like to play without.

Without heart, every day feels like a slog. No juice. Minutes and seconds are long. Relationships lack substance. Work lacks meaning. Life lacks a deeper burn. Scarcity surrounds us. There is no appetite for now, nor excitement for what's ahead.

With heart, every day is oozing with opportunity. Possibilities sit around every corner. Abundance is the theme of life. There is no doubt: life happens *for us* instead of *to us*. We look at a to-do-list with a Win Monday mindset of what we *get* to do, versus what we *have* to do. Bottom line: you feel alive, ready and armed with unshakable confidence.

In the upcoming chapters, you will meet heart-filled leaders who have mastered the green lights of **passion**, **authenticity**, **gratitude**, and **happiness**.

When these values are firing on all cylinders, life begins to take off as you are being true to your heart and everything within. This is where life happens on your terms, because you crafted it that way.

There are only two checkpoints en route to the Hands: your Head and your Heart.

The mind says go. Logic says green light.

Now, to complete the cycle of making better decisions faster and taking authentic action, we must harness our emotions and inner truth.

My experience in speaking and conversing about the head and heart during the writing of this book is that though both matter equally, people are far more aware of what's in their head; they are actively trying to find answers. The gap that many miss is that they're not using their hearts enough. This leads to anguish, a tamping down of the meaning inside us that, if openly shared, could transform our lives.

In our complex, constantly shifting society, we are told what we should believe, how we should behave, what we're missing out on, who is 100 percent right, and who is 100 percent wrong. All. The. Time. We hear it from advertisers, influencers, social media friends and foes, memes, politicians, and a constant line of people we don't even know. Even if we consciously avoid a lot of the noise, much of it still seeps through. As a result, I believe it has become increasingly difficult to listen to your own heart and trust what it's really saying.

I've already said it, and you'll hear more from me about this later in the book, but while head gaps and heart gaps are both real, in the modern world the heart gap is a more widespread problem for most of us. I'm telling you right now, if you're one of the many who struggles with it, you should *lead from your heart, because it's a forgotten art.*

You've absorbed enough on the head, for now. Time to dive into the second H, your heart, which by the end of the next four chapters will be central to all you do and who you are. Are you ready to:

- Ignite your passion?
- Shine a light on your authenticity?
- Be grateful for every moment and every day?
- Step into a state of inner happiness?

Heart will deliver on all, and then some.

PASSION

Ignite Your Burn

Your burn is the underlying fire that ignites your Why and Purpose.
—Ben Newman, elite performance coach

BEN NEWMAN HOSTS ONE of the most aptly named podcasts I've ever seen: *The Burn*. Ben is a highly sought-after performance coach, with clients that include the 18-time (and climbing) national champion Alabama Crimson Tide football team. He's also a #1 *Wall Street Journal* and *USA Today* bestselling author, consistently rated as a top global keynote speaker by Real Leaders, having been featured on NBC, ABC, CBS, Fox, ESPN, and in *Inc.*, *Forbes*, and the *Huffington Post*. I share this with you because Ben rarely talks about any of these accolades. He always comes back to a deeper burn.

It's your turn.

You are about to explore and experience the inner depths of your burn.

The burn that gets you out of bed. The burn to win Monday. The burn to become the best version of yourself. The burn that unlocks your maximum potential. The burn that lights your heart on fire.

In Ben's words, the burn is something we all have, but like a flaring green light that never sees the light of day, rarely do we uncover and connect to it.

Why?

Most often it's because we never take the time to examine what's in our heart and why it's in our heart. It could be a person you would do anything for or an eternal chip on your shoulder based on a doubter in your past; either way, it serves as the reason you step into each day with a burning passion that is palpable to everyone in your path.

If you're unclear what (or who) that is for you, this chapter will help reveal your burn so you can ignite your passion. With greater passion, better and faster decisions become inevitable.

You already know the drill. It's time to meet a few folks who are as passionate as they come, so we can all take a play from their playbooks and apply it to our lives. We start with a sports exec who has been a trailblazer in the industry from day one, with hunger (and humility) as her force multiplier. Then I'll introduce you to a top strength coach in the world, who will teach us how to break the needle—because moving the needle is for mere mortals.

Get ready for the burn!

Hunger x Humility: Your Force Multiplier

I don't use the word *trailblazer* lightly, but that's exactly what I think of when my dear friend Michele Kajiwara enters the room, a life, or an industry. A veteran climber at AEG, she is now the senior vice president of premium sales, service, and events at Crypto.com Arena (formerly Staples Center). In a career that started as a service manager, she grew to an executive level and is now responsible for five consecutive years of over $100 million in revenue for her team.

Her secret weapon? The ability to leverage hunger as her force multiplier.

"The hungrier you are," Michele shared on my podcast, "the more you get back, the more you engage, the more you network, the more you give—and not because there's an expectation that you're going to get something back. It naturally happens when you have this voracity for life, for work, for relationships, everything that you can give yourself to. It's impossible to not see hunger as an amplifier of all things good."

I hope you can literally feel the passion radiating from Michele, always leading from the heart, with a fire in her eye.

So how can we apply the same hunger to our lives?

I have good news, tough news, and great news.

- The good news: it can be cultivated.
- The tough news: it's really hard work.
- The great news: it's almost impossible to not be hungry when you're living with passion.

Back to Michele.

She believes in a yin-and-yang approach to hunger. Its counterpart is humility. When asked about why she's so passionate about life, she traces it back to her origins in Hawaii and the heart and spirit of aloha.

This grounded humility inspired by her closely knit family has been the igniter of her passion—because her humility is a constant reminder that there is much to appreciate in life—from nature to people and places and beyond. With this mindset, you never stop learning, growing, or being hungry. There is always something to be passionately curious about in each day. A perfect blend of head and heart.

I probed on this.

"If you want to spark hunger, you have to spark joy," she responded. "You have to tap into that little burning ember that makes you want to wake up before the sun and get to work, excited by what you might accomplish. That's where you'll find the resilience to overcome absolutely anything."

This theme of resilience is something I couldn't ignore.

"How do you maintain your drive to success when the worst happens?" I asked. Let's call it an economic crash.

"You stay humble," she replied. "You remember that nothing is just handed out, even in the best of times. You have to earn it now just as you did when things were flowing. Soon they'll start flowing again."

Those who are humble and hungry win, powered by unshakable confidence.

Just as Michele has earned many green lights, the same opportunity to win Monday and beyond is at your fingertips.

Before the upcoming Decision Drill, I have a confession to make:

When I met Michele over 15 years ago, she rejected me. Not in the way you might be thinking. Professionally, she took a hard pass on me to work for her team. Apparently, I was a red light!

Why?

Because I only had one of her core Hs. True to her values, if you're not humble and hungry, it's a nonstarter. I was as hungry as they came. As a young, successful sales guy, humility was not in the cards—and she called me on it. I was NOT the better decision. And trust me—she was fast!

Thankfully, I naturally developed my humility over time, and our relationship has blossomed ever since, but it wasn't without some humble pie—whether I liked it or not.

DECISION DRILL

In the rest of the chapter, the connection between passion and hunger will stay top of mind—so let's unpack humility a bit further.

Just like Michele took a hard pass on me, she also has shared her own red-light experiences of not getting the dream job or being passed on for an opportunity she felt she deserved. What advice does Michele have for all of us who have been in that same scenario?

"Look at who does get hired. Be self-aware. Don't sit and cry and say, 'Poor me.' Ask what you can improve so that next time an opportunity presents itself, you are the one that gets it."

Think of a time you were rejected, professionally or personally. Why did you get rejected? It's time to study your losses and take notes on what you can do for the next round so a *no* will become a *yes*.

To help you process this, put yourself in the other person's shoes and ask yourself why were you a red or yellow light to them?

In Michele's case, my lack of humility was a signal to her heart that she shouldn't hire me. Had I not had the skills, then her head would have been the driver of rejection.

Your turn. Why were you a red or yellow (from the other person's view) in this moment of rejection?

Notes: _____

_____

Based on what you just jotted down, decide what you will do different the next time.

Notes: _____

_____

Breaking the Needle

How do you find the strength to focus on a goal, identify what's essential, and use your focus to not only move the needle but move it so much that the needle breaks?

Jay Ferruggia is the master of this exact power.

Jay is host of the *Renegade Radio* podcast, a top-20 fitness podcast on Apple with over six million downloads, and he was also a humble and hungry guest on my podcast. Jay has been helping people become the strongest version of themselves since 1994, and today is heralded as a coach of coaches, trainer of trainers, and champion of mastering not only physical strength but emotional and mental strength as well. The perfect trifecta of head, heart, and hands! His work has appeared in *Men's Health*, *Muscle & Fitness*, *Fast Company*, *Huffington Post*, and *Entrepreneur*, as well as on ESPN and CBS.

Basically, when it comes to strength, he's got a knack. When you watch or listen to any of Jay's content, you'll clearly see, hear, and feel the passion. When he talks, rooms shake. The intensity is visible in his veins.

Jay is steadfast that in order to get where you want to go and build the life you ultimately want, you must break the needle.

At first hearing that, it sounds awesome. Break the needle. Absolutely! Got it!

Then I stepped back and asked myself, *What the hell does breaking the needle even mean?*

Instead of guessing, I asked Jay.

"The average person makes choices that move the needle," he said. "How can you become someone who generates so much momentum that you break the needle?"

Million-dollar question: **How do I break the needle?**

Jay's about to tell you.

Let's start with the most common advice we're all given about passion. Think of what you're passionate about. What do you love to do?

Guilty. I've said and asked this more times than I care to admit.

While Jay agrees with these thoughts in spirit, he disrupted them and did a 180.

"We always hear about build your life around the things you love, build your business around the things you love. But that's really hard to do because for me, I'm really passionate and intense, and I love a million things, so that list would be infinite. But instead of that, what about, what do you hate not doing?"

DECISION DRILL

Answer Jay's question. *What do you hate not doing?*

Put another way, what is a green light that you couldn't imagine yourself without?

In my case, I hate not being around people. I hate not watching sports. I hate not raising a glass with my closest friends and family. I hate not doing things that I feel make a difference. Flip the script, and this means I love teams, sports, good times, and driving impact in everything I do. I've now made a conscious decision to entrench these essentials in my life.

Your turn. What do you hate not doing?

Notes: _____

_____

_____

Sometimes, in order to find your passion, you must reverse engineer the process and rewire your mind to think about what you hate not doing versus what you love to do. Both are green lights. If you haven't already, fill out your notes above.

This brings us to a few other passion principles of Jay's—namely, nonnegotiables and minimalism.

Let's start with daily nonnegotiables.

Ask yourself: What's essential for your daily joy and progress?

From Jay's lens, take a look at your life and the things you're most passionate about. It might be exercise, spending time outside, or laughing. Make these things nonnegotiable as a part of your day. Better yet, make them a nonnegotiable part of your Monday. Set the tone for the week.

Need to make room for them? Decide to drop other things, but never the nonnegotiables that bring you joy and fuel your heart.

Now we connect to minimalism—or as Jay calls it, do more by doing less. "We all love to embrace the hustle of achieving 100 different things at a time. But the truth is that many of the people who have reached the pinnacle of success do it by focusing on one thing and doing that thing with everything they've got."

When Jay shared this, it was the gut punch I needed.

Like most, my plate is full. But am I maxing my productivity? Efficiency? Effectiveness?

The reality is, in the times where I've thrived most, it's because I had true focus and was ultra-decisive. I went head down on a project or series of tasks, progress and positive results followed, impact was maximized, and dare I say . . . mastery was formed. This is the sequence when I've decided to do more by doing less. I now have protected white space in my daily calendar, take self-retreats to reprioritize what's most important, journal my three nonnegotiables per day (starting with the hardest), all based on the perspective Jay and others have shared to embrace a minimalist lifestyle.

I'm still a work in progress, as we all are, but I found this to be incredibly valuable. I hope you will too.

Our Old Friend Curiosity

I believe there are two primary paths to passion: work and curiosity.

Work is based on the fact that most of us will work over 100,000 hours over the course of our careers. This is the biggest chunk of time we'll do ANYTHING; sleeping is a close runner-up. When we find passion in our work, it tends to carry over into the rest of our lives. *The litmus test: On a Sunday night, how do you feel about work Monday?* It's not easy to find these jobs of passion (I can help in this area; my contact details are at the end of the read), but passionate work creates passionate people who tend to lead more passionate lives—a trifecta of making better decisions faster and with maximum confidence.

The second takes us back to our last chapter, "Curiosity." Start with what you're curious about and you can discover clues toward your passion. It's no coincidence this is how many *passion projects* start. People lean into what they're most curious about, they invest time in it, they experiment, they iterate. Sometimes it stays a side-hustle, other times it's an ALL-IN entrepreneurial journey, and still other times it's a swing and a miss. But every attempted green that turns out yellow or red better informs us what the next ideal green should look like. *This might remind you of dating!*

If all else fails, start with curiosity. Through this path, we find passion in life, hopefully passion at work. The payout: we *feel* alive.

TO RECAP PASSION:

1. **Allow hunger and humility to be your force multiplier.** Both fuel and truth to the heart. A heart that will lead to better decisions faster.

2. **Like our main man, Jay, don't move the needle—break it.** Ask yourself what green lights you hate not doing and do more of them.

Do this, and you will live on your terms—as long as you embrace our next value, authenticity.

For bonus content on Passion, scan the QR code to tap into the keys of what intrinsically motivates you, taught by a health-and-wellness juggernaut garnering media attention around the globe.

AUTHENTICITY

Give Up Your Terms,
Give Up Your Life

*Authenticity is the daily practice of letting go of who we think we're
supposed to be and embracing who we are.*
—Brené Brown, six-time *New York Times* #1 bestselling author

I SOLD OUT.

Unquestionably, this was the moment I hit rock bottom in my
professional career.

After years of thinking I was doing it right—career thriving, LinkedIn
profile polished and pristine, dream career, results never in doubt—I
thought I had it all.

This was the performance review that woke me up to the harsh
reality that I was doing it all wrong.

I was told my team doesn't think I care about them.

IMPOSSIBLE. Care is my calling card.

I actually mean it when I say *people first*.

How could it be?

Turns out my heart cared, but my decisions and actions didn't show it—and that's all that mattered to our team.

The gap . . .

. . . was authenticity.

Authenticity is who you are *and* how you show up—combined.

You can say you're honest, but do you live it? Having a core value of integrity, saying your honest, then telling the whole truth 80 percent of the time just doesn't cut it.

Head + Heart = Hands is always a combo meal.

While the full details of my rock-bottom performance review are in my first book, I had to kick off a chapter on authenticity with this story because it shows my authenticity at its worst. This admission is a balanced blend of vulnerability and authenticity.

You may be thinking, *Relax, Paul. It was just one review*. Wrong. It was a callout of years of moments of inauthentic behavior and poor decisions that prioritized corporate goals over being my true self.

The worst part . . .

Authenticity is one of my five core values.

How's that for a gut punch?

When you give up your values, you give up your terms, and you give up your life.

Because authenticity is the portal to this entire equation and set of values. Authenticity endorses the *better* in better decisions faster.

Think about it. If these green lights serve as fuel to your head, heart, and hands, the ongoing test is whether you are *authentically* expressing:

- **growth**
- **positivity**
- **grit** '
- **curiosity**
- **passion**
- **authenticity**
- **gratitude**
- **happiness**
- **courage**
- **service**
- **excellence**
- **impact**

Real (authentic) growth versus fake growth.

Real positivity versus fake positivity.

Real grit versus fake grit.

You get the drift.

Real and authentic wins. It's not even close.

Here we are. It's halftime of the big game.

As the road map reflects, this is the midway checkpoint. You're entering the sixth of 12 chapters on green-light values.

Are you willing and ready to commit to live these 12 greens every day? Not when you feel like it. Not when convenient. EVERY day, kicking off Monday, of course.

If you are, a more purposeful life of authenticity, unshakable confidence, and better decisions faster awaits.

One of the world's leading motivational speakers, Eric Thomas, says, "When you want to succeed as bad as you want to breathe, then you'll be successful."

When done right, authenticity can be your oxygen. When *being real* is on proud display and it's coming from the heart, you breathe easier, sleep easier, love easier, work easier, and live easier.

Life won't always be easy, but it will be easier. Because authenticity is simple once you decide to be a single you. Not different versions of work you, home you, social you—just YOU.

Let's welcome our cast of authenticity. We kick off with someone who ran revenue for the 2022 Super Bowl in Los Angeles, but way more important in my eyes is one of the best-hearted people I know. Then we meet an entrepreneur who appeared on *Shark Tank* only to realize her biggest mission was larger than a company—or shark—could ever make it.

Fired up for you all to meet.

Finding Strength in Vulnerability

I'm in the Owner's Club at AT&T Stadium, home of the Dallas Cowboys. The setting: an annual retreat for Legends, a global sports consulting company owned by the Cowboys, Yankees, and others.

The topic: leadership.

The speaker: Greg Kish, now head of revenue at SoFi Stadium, then in a sales leadership role at the 49ers.

I *kind of* knew Greg at the time. Beers, friendly support, sharing of best practices, the usual industry relationship you would expect.

When he took the stage, I anticipated hearing the same old corporate talk about leadership (sans heart), which unfortunately was just that—talk.

But Greg immediately said something that spoke to me.

When asked what the #1 key to leadership is, he said: *authenticity*.

He went on to share family stories of how being genuine has shown up in his life, has served him positively in many ways, and has been kryptonite he's seen in others, including personally on his worst day.

While I didn't know what was to come, that speech turned out to have a massive impact on me and our relationship. Within years, a green light and better, faster decision led me to partner with Greg at the 49ers, where we did some incredible work together. You could say our hands joined forces because our hearts aligned. It also didn't hurt that we philosophically saw business the same way in our heads. 3H synergy at its finest.

Most importantly, likely because of this authentic synergy, I am proud to call Greg (a.k.a. Kish) a close friend and somebody I would do anything for.

We bonded over authenticity. It's one of the core values and traits that gets us out of bed. It's our oxygen, and consequently, it's how we measure others, with the standard always in the mirror. We always joke it's only hard to be authentic when you have to question whether you're being authentic.

To the best of our abilities, Greg and I have consistently strived to be unapologetically ourselves. What you see is what you get. There's only one version. Imperfections included.

While I certainly didn't need a podcast conversation to learn more about Greg, I had him on anyway!

In our convo, he talked about his keys to leadership. Of course, authenticity was included. He followed on with care, consistency, vulnerability, and awareness.

From Greg's lens, where there's self-awareness, there's strength. If you recall, awareness is a table stake of our Win Monday Community.

When you're aware of always being authentic, you show up consistently and confidently, you're comfortable being vulnerable, and it will naturally show others you care—not about them as a producer but as a whole person. That's leadership—and this is Greg's formula to be your most authentic self. This is why he's been so successful: he stays true to these core tenets.

On the surface, the world applauds Greg's accomplishments as a sales leader in three of the most iconic sports venues in industry history. To me, he's just Greg. The same authentic dude who skateboards through South Bay LA, loves hanging with his family at the beach, has a daughter who is a killer soccer player, knows how to grill with the best of them, will always take a dive bar over anything posh, picked up meditating during the pandemic—and oh yeah, he runs revenue for a $5 billion venue. Greg doesn't have to change who he is to thrive at work, and that's something we can all aspire to.

Ask Greg about his measurement of success (and significance).

He'll tell you it's serving as a catalyst to help others become the best version of themselves and maximize their potential. Coach, leader, purpose driver—those are the titles that matter to him at work. No doubt, dad and husband will always rise above that.

What unlocked this holistic lifestyle for him?

One word: *vulnerability*.

Once he decided to become vulnerable, authenticity was waiting on the other side.

When I asked Greg why more people don't show their vulnerability, he admitted, "There was a time where vulnerability was seen as a weakness. Now we understand it's really a superpower. It builds trust in others when we reveal our vulnerabilities."

That's the power of vulnerable truths.

Your turn.

DECISION DRILL

Write down one thing most people don't know about you that you consider to be a vulnerable truth. Think of this as a truth in your heart that your head hasn't opened you up to share with others.

_____

It's time to take this yellow to a green.

Think of one person you're willing to share this with in the coming weeks. Go beyond your comfort zone. This will only be impactful if it's something they don't already know or they will be somewhat surprised you told them. Most importantly, sharing this has the opportunity to bring your relationship closer together.

Write their name down below and text them to say you want to catch up.

_____

Schedule a coffee meet, Zoom, or something else—you do you. If you like, you might make this a regular (I recommend biweekly or monthly) practice.

Authenticity requires vulnerability. Better decisions faster requires vulnerability. Vulnerability unmasks the greens that were always there, hiding, until now.

The Risk of Not Taking Risks

I gotta admit, as an avid fan of *Shark Tank*, I was pretty geeked up to chat with Kelsey Moreira. The founder and fearless leader of Doughp, a mission-driven edible and bakeable cookie dough business that led to her being named to *Forbes'* 30 under 30, Kelsey appeared on *Shark Tank* looking for that life-changing green light.

If the intro stopped there, you'd say, "Awesome! She sounds doughp."

The reality is, we haven't even scratched the surface of what makes Kelsey so successful, impactful, or authentic.

When I asked about some of her earliest insights, she shared a thought-provoking connection between personal growth and building a business.

Kelsey believes that you are your most powerful product, so you need to embrace the authentic ability to sell yourself. We're not all going to be on *Shark Tank*. We don't all have an amazing product. But what we do have is the ability to sell ourselves, to sell a dream, and to sell the best possible version of our authentic self—to partners, teams, family, friends, clients, and everyone we meet.

Most of us (not in sales) would feel a risk of judgment and anxiety at the thought of selling ourselves to others, especially on a daily basis.

But Kelsey remains steadfast that the ability to sell yourself is the threshold of stepping into your most authentic space. At first it may be awkward. With practice, it can become a permanent strength.

DECISION DRILL

How would you describe the best (most authentic) version of yourself?

Notes: _____

_____

Think of one person (or group of people) where you're doing a great job showing up as this person. Your energy and mood is bright green when you're around them.

Who is this person/this group of people? _____

Stay consistent, don't let up.

Now think of one person (or group of people) you have *not* consistently been showing up as this person, but you would like to. Unfortunately, they see the red and yellow side of you. But that stops today!

Who is this person/this group of people? _____

What is your next step to change the dynamic of how they authentically view you? _____

_____

The tough news: This will initially be difficult.

The great news: Showing up at your best is required to consistently make better decisions faster. Follow this playbook and you're well on your way to acing this drill.

Is there risk in being authentic and FULLY opening up with others? I suppose that depends on your lens.

Are you looking at it from other people's point of view? Or yours?

Often when we rise above the outside noise (where the perceived risk is letting other people's opinions influence what we do or don't do), authenticity becomes more available and abundant because it's being sourced from our heart, fully on our terms—nobody else's.

This is exactly what happened in Kelsey's case.

There were some skeletons in her closet, pre-Doughp. She was a fast riser in Silicon Valley, working around the clock. Alcohol became a theme, and it took a toll—physically, mentally, and emotionally.

It wasn't until she sobered up, left tech, and founded Doughp that her most significant impact emerged.

While many know her as the queen of the cookie dough business, she didn't start the company pursuing world cookie dough domination. On the contrary, there was a more authentic cause.

Her bigger mission is to reduce social stigmas around addiction recovery and mental health—based on her own personal struggles. This is the narrative she has chosen to put out to the world—taking risk by sharing her greatest pains in order to help end the suffering of others. The risk is worth it because it's authentically on her terms.

Doughp was never solely about the balance sheets. The amplifier it needed was the decision to stand for something bigger than a product.

It wasn't until Kelsey allowed her experience with mental health and sobriety to influence her customers for the better that she realized its true potential—as a business with purpose. From donating portions of every sale to recovery foundations to "walking the walk" through mental health days and talking with her community about the *tough stuff*, Kelsey has truly created a business that has become a force for good—for countless people who are struggling and just needed a safe outlet.

This is the epitome of a Head + Heart = Hands business that makes better decisions faster, time and time again.

Kelsey wakes up every day to take a risk and be true to her mission, because there's a massive risk in not taking risks.

Happy Wife, Authentic Life

I posted the following on social media:

> *3 years of long-distance can be an absolute grind - but we wouldn't be where we are without it. Call it the biggest test in life. The biggest sacrifice. The biggest builder of trust, connection, empathy, compassion, understanding, and love . . .*
>
> *The most valuable lesson I learned from these 36 months from 2011–2014 was how intentional life can be, when you are where your feet are, you eliminate outside noise, and fully focus on the person in front of you. Long-distance, it was easier. Now together every day since, it's harder.*
>
> *In 2022, I'm recommitting to be like 'long distance Paul' because I couldn't imagine my life without [my wife], and she deserves the best version of myself. Cheers to the hard road ahead, because every moment is so precious, and so worth it.*
>
> *Happy Valentine's Day Mayra!*

Our wedding vows were similar. I shared how easy it is to be with her—because of her authenticity—and she saw mine. When right, you mold into one another. You don't need to make sweeping or drastic changes. Be you, and the right people will authentically accept you for that.

Come to think of it, the best working relationships I've had with people and teams have been the exact same. Authenticity may have cost me some people over the years, but it's never cost me the right ones.

Wishing you the same in your life. **Authenticity wins**.

TO RECAP AUTHENTICITY:

1. **Self-awareness and vulnerability are the keys to authenticity**. Unmask the greens that are waiting to happen by sharing a vulnerable truth with one person today. Scary, but awesome.
2. **There is a risk in not taking risk.** Your head may be wired to not take risk, so lead with your heart to battle through (and overcome) the yellows. *Cool idea: do one heart-led act every Monday.*

An authentic life is one filled with gratitude. That's our next stop on the *Better Decisions Faster* journey.

For (2x) bonus content on Authenticity, scan the QR code to learn how to cultivate authentic green-light relationships.

GRATITUDE

Get to Do Beats Have to Do

This a wonderful day. I've never seen this one before.—Maya Angelou

WHEN I STARTED TO journal what I *get* to do versus what I *have* to do, my day-to-day energy and attitude transformed. It's been one of the best and fastest decision shifts of my life.

The simplest task becomes special. The mundane has meaning. Obligations turn to opportunities. Activities present possibilities.

When every element of the day becomes a *get* to do, gratitude is impossible to ignore.

The beauty of gratitude . . . it's a choice.

The moment it hit for me, which I detailed in my first book, is when I did a virtual webinar (yes, ANOTHER Zoom meeting) for Major League Baseball's Oakland Athletics sales team. The talk was about applying purpose to daily business and life. Shortly after our session, the VP of sales sent a note thanking me, saying that his 16- and 18-year-old sons (who overheard my talk while they were home from school because of the early pandemic quarantine) approached him and said, "Dad, can we talk about our purpose?"

That's all I needed to hear.

Instead of *having* to do ANOTHER webinar (red- or yellow-light mentality), I got to touch a few special lives in a way that would have never happened had there been no pandemic. If they're in school, we likely do our session in person, and life goes on without them asking for that green-light conversation with Dad.

I'll never look at a webinar the same. If you can touch one life or connect deeper with one person, what an amazing thing to *get* to do. I urge you to enter every meeting going forward with this mindset and heartset. You decide how you show up, Monday and beyond.

I now journal one thing I *get* to do every day so that gratitude is guaranteed. At minimum, that's 365 doses of gratitude per year. You'll find you won't stop at one per day. Hell of a recipe, if you ask me.

In this chapter, multiple leaders in life will inspire gratitude in us all. We kick off with a grounding perspective of being where your feet are with somebody who I consider to be on the Mount Rushmore of sports and entertainment industry titans, to then meet a well-traveled south-side Chicago-born Harvard alum turned Silicon Valley inclusion executive who will help you build your identity toolbox. Cherry on top, if you've ever enjoyed Hint water, you'll meet their founder too.

Be Where Your Feet Are

Say hello to Scott O'Neil.

Bestselling author of *Be Where Your Feet Are*, Scott has more than 20 years of experience in the NBA, NHL, and NFL and has earned a reputation as a leader of leaders. Now CEO of Merlin Entertainments, formerly serving as CEO of the Philadelphia 76ers and New Jersey Devils, he's also been president of Madison Square Garden and senior vice president at the NBA league office. He has made countless 40-under-40 lists, including *Adweek* and *Sporting News*, while also being tabbed as one of the most influential people, innovative executives, and admired CEOs in America. He's appeared on CNN, CNBC, Fox Business, and even cohosted multiple shows on Bloomberg Television. He has a passion for company culture like none other, with his latest mission to inspire others to be where their feet are.

When Scott talks about being where your feet are, here's what he means—directly from his book summary:

> *When we're moving at 115 MPH, we rarely see the wall coming. But it comes for all of us and when it does, we grasp for lessons, for meaning, for purpose. Each moment (good or bad) and each win or loss, provides us an opportunity to learn, and if we choose to take it, that opportunity can change our lives—and the world— for the better. The human spirit craves connection. Authenticity. Belonging. Touch.* **Gratitude.** *Purpose. We need to make our interactions count. Whether it's the death of a friend, loss of a job, a bad break-up, or the isolation of Covid-19, those who manage to be where their feet are will grow, stretch and emerge stronger, smarter and more prepared as we find peace and gratitude in the pause.*

Couldn't think of a better place for each of us to pause, right now, in gratitude.

DECISION DRILL

Time to take a breath and ask yourself:

What are five green-light decisions you've made that you are truly grateful for?

Possibilities range from relationships, partnerships, friends, career choices, health commitments, personal growth, and so on. List the five green-light decisions below.

1. _____

2. _____

3. _____

4. _____

5. _____

There is much to be grateful for, especially when we pause. Create a ritual right now to decide and commit to a daily practice of gratitude. Some of us journal, others have a reminder pop up on our phone, others carry an index card in their pocket of what they're grateful for, and others share their gratitude practice with another person to let them know they're grateful for their relationship. From a text to a five-minute sit-down routine at the beginning or end of the day, most important is that gratitude is baked into each day. There is no right or perfect way to do it. The only wrong is *not* doing it.

A member of our Win Monday Community recently shared they do the decision drill you just completed weekly. Every Monday they do a gratitude green-light journal for the week that was, and the week to come. This allows her to balance a daily lens with a bigger (but still within view) weekly lens.

Back to Scott.

He believes in three daily components we should practice to achieve full presence in day-to-day life.

- Do something for your mind, body, and soul every day.
- Practice gratitude.
- Put your phone down. Get out and exercise.

The foundation of a full and fulfilling life lies in these simple building blocks.

Another lesson I learned from Scott in a recent conversation came from a similar pain point we share. We both have a self-admitted weakness of overextending and overcommitting ourselves based on not being able to say no. *Sound familiar?*

As an example, an industry colleague asks Scott to spend 10 minutes on a mentoring call with their son or daughter. Of course, he says yes. That's fine if there's one ask. But what if there are 20 asks in a day? Sounds extreme, but this is reality for many.

For me, the challenge is saying yes to every project or shiny idea that excites me. While it fuels me, it ends up draining me more in the long run because I have no more energy to pour out—at times to the people who matter most or to the activities that can drive the most impact.

Worse yet, we ourselves are often the person we hurt the most. Scott shared that sentiment.

His perspective was to fix your scaffolding.

Want to serve others? Start with a strong foundation.

Serving the people around us is like standing on a scaffolding to complete a project. If our own scaffolding is shaky, we can't be as effective. Sometimes we have to make the decision and take the time to improve ourselves before we can truly serve others.

The gratitude practice from the last decision drill is a phenomenal place to start in service of self, to be where our feet are, fulfill our potential, and live confidently by leading with gratitude.

Your Identity Toolbox

Identity.

So important yet so little clarity in understanding what it truly is.

What if you were moments away from being clear on how to more effectively explore your identity? I could argue this clarity is one of the most valuable things in the world to be grateful for.

You are indeed moments away and it comes in the form of an identity toolbox, shared by one of the warmest hearts I know, Torian Richardson.

Torian is the Head of Global Inclusive Recruiting for NVIDIA, one of Silicon Valley's most innovative and thriving companies. He also wears hats as an investor, growth advisor, board director, culture scientist, and global executive coach. While Harvard alum is a part of his bio, Torian lights up even more when he speaks of his other university: Tsinghua, in Beijing, China.

Well-traveled would be the understatement of the century when it comes to Torian, as he's visited 70 countries and worked on four continents through his 20-plus years of leadership. Torian is a firm believer in lifelong learning through experience and immersion. He's intellectually curious and never complacent, has an awesome attitude, takes ownership of outcomes, and is all about consistent decisions and actions to do well—and do good. Head, heart, and hands fully aligned.

This is why I place such high value on Torian's unique lens when it comes to shaping our internal beliefs on identity and external beliefs on gratitude.

Torian suggests that we each have an identity toolbox. Your toolbox has three vital elements—purpose, variety, and relationships.

Your *purpose* is your reason, the way you take internal inspiration and transform it into action. *Variety* is how you expand the horizons of your own experiences, pushing you into environments that are uncomfortable and help you grow. *Relationships* are the amplifier beyond ourselves.

Purpose, variety, and relationships all combine to build our capacity and what we're capable of achieving. But Torian warns us this process won't just happen. It needs to be intentionally developed each day by the decisions and actions we take. Torian's favorite quote is from Benjamin Franklin: "Well done is better than well said."

"The people that pivot from inspiration to decisive action are the ones who really affect change," he said. "Consistent action leads to progress in ways that procrastination never will."

Another benefit of action is the learning that takes place from it, as Torian has discovered through his immersion and deep travels. I recently asked him about his top lessons and insights gathered from all these distant cultures, and why he's emerged so grateful for it.

Here are just two highlights:

1. **There is power in saying "I don't know."** We often think that having all the answers is strength or subscribe to the "fake it

till you make it" camp. When you're on foreign soil, that's not an option. You truly don't know how things are done or how people live. So you strip yourself down and become "courageously vulnerable," as Torian calls it. It takes courage to be vulnerable. On your home turf, vulnerability can be challenging. Overseas where you may not even speak the language, vulnerability is the cost of entry. As a bonus, it can also be great perspective on how to be grateful for the blessings we have in our home environment. *Are we reminding ourselves of this gratitude every day?*

2. **Find common ground**. At times Torian had to conquer the feeling of being the odd one out. While he considers diversity far beyond the color of our skin, Torian is African American, and a large part of his story is based on his years in China, where as he says it, "there ain't another brother around until the next continent over."

"When you feel like there's a wall between you and everyone else, it's easy to withdraw into yourself," he said. "But the path forward is through that wall, insisting on finding ways to identify with all kinds of people. Broaden your experiences even when it's difficult and watch how your life is transformed."

When he was in China, he said externally he had little in common with the people there. So he asked himself, *What do we have in common? What is the perceived red that can be flipped into a green?* All of a sudden, a connection around food and family surfaced. Then conversation around culture and rituals. Relationships formed and blossomed thereafter. When you find common ground, you realize gratitude for what we share can be a powerful unifier.

Torian's insights aren't limited to cross-cultural encounters. He takes seriously the much more personal act of forgiveness.

DECISION DRILL

Forgiveness releases us from limits on our potential.

Regret is a weight around our necks, strangling the possibility of better decisions faster. It stalls our momentum and requires us to work harder than we should to grow and improve ourselves. One thing the identity toolbox doesn't have room for is regret or resentment—forgive yourself, forgive others, and reach your fullest potential.

Who is one person you need to forgive? What red-light encounter do you need to forgive them for? _____

_____

_____

In the mirror, what is one thing you can forgive yourself for?

_____

_____

Give yourself grace and unleash that long overdue green light to self.

A Grateful Close

Kara Goldin, founder of Hint Water and bestselling author of *Undaunted*, is an absolute rock star. Accolades range from *InStyle*'s

Badass 50, Fast Company's Most Creative People in Business, *Fortune*'s Most Powerful Women Entrepreneurs, to the *Huffington Post* listing her as one of six disruptors in business, alongside Steve Jobs and Mark Zuckerberg.

Yet what I found most impressive in my conversation with Kara was her humility and gratitude for where she is and what she's been through.

She's faced countless obstacles and had every door slammed in her face, from 40 percent of her business disappearing overnight based on a sudden shift in Starbucks strategy to a Coke executive calling her *sweetie* and telling her this "unsweetened flavored water thing" will never work. She had every opportunity to fold, shut it down, or never even get started. But she's now (and forever will be) a proud founder of a $250 million annual business of a product you've likely enjoyed. Kara remains undaunted and says we always have a choice—a choice to walk away OR a decision to be grateful that life seems to become clear over time when you take action and stay grateful regardless of the circumstances around you.

When crisis happens, did it happen *to* you or *for* you? In Kara's eyes, everything happens for you, and everything has a purpose, if you allow it and confidently embrace it.

TO RECAP GRATITUDE:

1. **Be where your feet are**. Practice gratitude daily. Green lights and better decisions faster await.
2. **Find common ground and make relationships a top priority in life**. You can only be your best self when you surround yourself with like-minded and like-hearted people.

3. **_Bonus from Kara Goldin_: remain undaunted in your pursuit of gratitude and _get_ (not _have_) to dos.** This is when life happens _for_ you, not _to_ you.

Once your heart is grateful, a path is paved for happiness—from the inside out.

For bonus content on Gratitude, scan the QR code below to access a daily journal exercise from my first book that goes beyond gratitude to also inspire daily excitement.

HAPPINESS

Cracking the Happiness Code

Success without fulfillment is failure.
—Tony Robbins

THIS CHAPTER IS AS much about cracking the happiness code as it is about fulfillment.

Why?

Because true fulfillment is inner success, authentic happiness, and living with significance.

When you combine all these ingredients, I believe there are two types of happiness. Happiness we outwardly express (whether it's real or made up) and happiness we *feel* on the inside—starting in our heart.

The outside version shows up as a smile regardless of whether you're happy. It's unfortunately become commonplace in today's times. The problem is, it's internally dangerous. It can lead to feelings where we have to "keep up with the Joneses" or "imposter syndrome." We get pulled into this vicious trap because of outside forces like other people's opinions or social media. Negative decisions and actions often follow.

What started as a dopamine hit when somebody liked your post leads to the steady scroll of death. A scroll where you see the top 1 percent of people's lives (filtered, of course) always smiling, then you compare yourself to them and say I want to be there, I want to do that, or worse yet, I want to be them. You feel worse exiting the scroll of death than you were excited to scratch the itch and click on the app.

No judgment; we've all been there. But that smile you see on a screen is too often just a smoke screen. You, too, have probably seen families eating out at dinner tables posing for that perfect picture, then one minute later they're arguing, glued to their phones, or not even talking—for the rest of the evening. Woof.

This chapter doesn't focus on *fake* happy. If we're going to crack the code, we have to focus on *real* happy. Authentic happy. The happy that sticks and transforms into lasting joy. The happy that leads to vitality, better health—mental, emotional, and physical—and, of course, better decisions faster.

I'll soon introduce you to someone who became known as the female Jerry Maguire, inspired by a red-to-green leap. From there, you'll meet one of the first employees at a start-up—before it was a household name and used in every household and office—whose mission was to deliver happiness. You may have heard of them.

Zoom Video.

Time to crack the code.

I'll Be Happy When . . .

Imagine you could be equally excited about the future as you are grateful and happy with the present. Sue Izzo is the expert at this balance—or should I say, harmony.

Sue is a highly accomplished sports agent and manager known by many as the female Jerry Maguire. She owned a successful sports management agency for 17 years, where she represented Olympic athletes, X Games gold medalists, world champion surfers, and TV personalities. She has also been an executive producer of entertainment properties for ESPN, ABC, Apple TV, and NBC. Through a variety of experiences, she (like me) decided to take a Jerry Maguire leap from a robust career into her calling of coaching others to allow for more freedom and green lights in their business and lives.

While many moments led up to this leap, one of the more impactful was when Sue fell into the external happiness trap.

As Sue shared on my podcast, "I'll be happy when I get this deal. I'll be happy when my athlete wins the Olympic medal. I'll be happy when we get this entertainment project. And it was one day in the office when one of my employees turned to me and she said, 'You realize you always say that, and you're never happy.' And it hit like a ton of bricks. I was like, 'Oh my stars.' She was so right. I was living my whole existence on the next, 'I'll be happy when.'"

Have you ever experienced an "I'll be happy when . . ." moment?

Highly likely.

For me, I lost count.

DECISION DRILL

It's time for the truth serum. Those red lights you likely never speak about . . . because you thought they'd be greens.

Think about the times you've said, "I'll be happy when . . ." professionally or personally.

Professional can be (but not limited to) that big raise, promotion, new company where the grass should be greener. Personal can be the house, car, vacation . . . the list goes on.

Let's jot some examples of your own.

Be REAL. This exercise has infinitely more impact if you go to a space of vulnerability, maybe even pain, where you thought you'd be happy and then weren't. The letdown was disappointing at best, crushing and demoralizing at worst. List your examples below.

Professional
I'll be happy when . . . _____

_____

Personal
I'll be happy when . . . _____

_____

Bonus Round—One More (Professional or Personal)
I'll be happy when . . . _____

_____

Now that you've (positively) exposed yourself in this Decision Drill, know that you have company. Every reader of this book, every member of the Win Monday Community, Sue—we've all been there.

Right after this chapter, you'll read my personal struggle with the external happiness trap; it got pretty ugly.

Back to Sue.

She found herself caught in the trap of thinking (and deciding) that her happiness and fulfillment were just one accomplishment or achieved goal away. "The truth is that happiness has far less to do with our achievements and successes and a whole lot more to do with your mindset," she shared. "Decide to have joy today; don't wait until tomorrow."

When she reframed it this way, it reminded me a lot of our gratitude practices. Why wait to be grateful until tomorrow when we can focus on what we get to be grateful for today?

The same applies to happiness—it is at your fingertips right now.

Another mic drop moment from Sue was how the little things are usually the ones that matter most.

"We always think that joy in life comes from the big moments, but in reality, it comes from all the tiny events that make us human," she said. "A kind interaction at the grocery store. A phone call from a loved one. A beautiful spring morning. Don't miss out on those moments with your head fixated on future massive events."

Sue and I are as guilty as anybody of this external or future-focused happiness trap.

We also see it with our clients all the time. We've been blessed to coach pro athletes, entertainers, and executives, and now understand that the correlation between wealth and happiness is minimal. We believe having more things, staying at the fancy hotel, or living in a nicer place will elevate our happiness, when that's factually not the case, as research has shown. A study by Princeton University states that the correlation of more money leading to more happiness ends at about the $75,000 mark.* Anything above that, there is no positive connection. In other words, mo' money ($\neq$) mo' happiness.

Which proves the point that true happiness starts within—and a great first step to implement this in your life is to reframe future-based versions of "I'll be happy when . . ." (artificial red lights) to current-based "I *am* happy because . . ." (true green lights). Give it a quick shot.

I am happy because . . . _____

_____

You can have goals, ambitions, and desires for the future; just don't attach them to happiness. Want those things because they fuel the other green lights in the *Better Decisions Faster* journey like growth and passion. Happiness is a now thing, not a future thing.

Give the "I am happy because . . ." exercise a shot, maybe even insert it in your daily journaling or Win Monday routine.

Do it, and you'll be well on your way to cracking the happiness code.

Delivering Happiness

Greg Holmes is the former head of sales for Zoom Video, one of the most astonishing success stories in tech and beyond. But Greg began his career as a schoolteacher, and the lessons he learned there—as well as those he learned when jumping headfirst into uncharted territory—helped him transform Zoom into the videoconferencing powerhouse it is today.

Their mission from day one: deliver happiness.

Zoom founder and CEO Eric Yuan, who wrote the foreword for *The Power of Playing Offense*, brought Greg in as one of the first handful

---

* Belinda Luscombe, "Do We Need $75,000 a Year to Be Happy?," *TIME*, September 6, 2010, https://content.time.com/time/magazine/article/0,9171,2019628,00.html.

of employees. It was Eric, a few engineers, and Greg—borne from their prior experiences together at Webex. They knew there was a better (faster) way to deliver happiness to all stakeholders on the inside and out. From team members to community to customers, they all matter—because everybody deserves to be happy. When happiness happens, business wins—and so do people.

Knowing the explosive growth Zoom had experienced, I had Greg on my podcast's inaugural episode (then called the *Playmakers* podcast, now the *Win Monday* podcast) to see how we could all learn from the playbook of delivering happiness at scale. Some of the insights surprised; others confirmed and validated.

Greg, like me, is a steadfast believer that happiness and fulfillment are the metrics that matter. It then becomes a game of how we can harness the balance between success and achievement to reach them.

In Greg's words, "When you deliver happiness, you receive success." A classic case of green begets green.

One way he brought that to life was in his interview process.

"Interviewing potential employees or partners about their skills, experience, and other factors is important," Greg said. "But the most important question is this: Are they committed to delivering happiness to our customers and audience? Because if they deliver happiness, our customers will reward us with their committed loyalty for life."

This is a prime example of a heart-based strategy and dedication to the company's mission. Knowing Greg and Zoom as a client and partner, it's something I'd expected to hear.

Then we started to drill deeper. Less corporate. More raw.

We peeled the onion and got down to Greg's true essence, where the inner teacher of kindness and compassion emerged.

I asked him how to cultivate happiness from scratch, especially when we're not in a happy place in a given moment.

He suggested to take it day by day. Decision by decision.

"Wake up today, smile, then try to go do it again tomorrow," he said. "The world is a mess. Facing it with a smile isn't a matter of who or where you are; it's a habit that you have to develop like any other. The first time you wake up and force a smile will be difficult, the second will be less difficult, and the one hundredth time will be second nature."

Note that this is *not* the artificial smile previously referenced. That's to please others. This smile is for yourself because you believe it will lead to better results, confidence, and fulfillment if you create a habit of smiling from within.

These same lessons apply to a classroom, home, or boardroom.

Greg has been building this happiness habit for years and admitted that it's now almost become a sixth sense. When he sees that others aren't happy, he decides to step in. It's what he used to do in school; he then did it at Zoom's headquarters. He developed a sense for when others are in need.

"Find opportunities to lift and help others and you'll never have a day without meaning and purpose," he said. "Develop a 'sixth sense' of when people around you are going through things, seeking ways to help them. Everyone needs a hand to help them through the crazy challenges of life."

His advice to us all on how to develop this sixth sense: seek random acts of kindness and discover how your life changes.

Every random act of kindness begins with a decision. Amazing how simple it is to Win Monday by choosing to do something, no matter how small it may seem. A heart-led example from Greg's experience is to simply pay the car toll for the person behind you. It's that simple. They'll never know you did it, and no one else will either, but that's not the point. These small acts of meaning are the things that bring life purpose and authentic happiness.

DECISION DRILL

Commit to one decision of kindness—from the heart.

What will it be? _____

When are you doing it? _____

A great way to think about it is if it were this person's birthday.
How would you want them to feel? What can you do to make it
a birthday moment they'll never forget?

Jot your notes above and make this green light happen.

P.S.—you can always treat somebody like it's their birthday.

What's the latest on Greg?

He decided to step away from the grind.

What he has found is a powerful perspective on what matters most.
His family, his passions, and the opportunity to help others. Those
are the things he's pursuing today.

As Greg shared, "Taking some time to figure out where you stand
relative to your vision for your life is a powerful thing."

I'm proud to call Greg an authentic friend. A great human being
with a heart of gold.

He's finding happiness in other things beyond work. How long will
this period last? Who knows—and he's not worried about it.

He's focused on being happy, one Monday, one decision, and one green light at a time.

Proud of you, Greg.

Don't Bypass the Heart

Happiness is the perfect finale for heartset.

Just like you know when you're authentically happy, your heart knows when your heart is true and on board. No convincing needed. No sugarcoating. No second guessing. No BS. You know when you know.

A reminder to lead from your heart, because it's a forgotten art . . . in a world that's largely driven by the head. More on this in the summary conclusion of *Better Decisions Faster*.

TO RECAP HAPPINESS:

1. **Beware of the external happiness trap**. Replace "I'll be happy when . . ." with "I *am* happy because . . ." These are the green lights and the way to better decisions faster today.

2. **Deliver happiness to everyone you touch**. Random heartfelt acts of kindness can go a long way, especially when others are down. Not everyone loves Mondays—what a great opportunity.

As we wrap the second H in the Head + Heart = Hands Equation, green lights are dialed in:

Passion ☑   Gratitude ☑

Authenticity ☑   Happiness ☑

While the upcoming part on Hands will talk about the purposeful outcomes and results of aligning our head, heart, and hands, thanks to the last two sections (head and heart), the critical components to understand whether we should take authentic action are now in the rearview mirror.

Head ☑
Heart ☑

Let's proceed to our final H, Hands, but first a vulnerable story that highlights how happiness connects to inner success, significance, and fulfillment, including the pitfalls and pain of an experience of mine that I've never written until now.

See you on the other side.

For bonus content on Happiness, scan the QR code below to access the first podcast I ever hosted. I was joined by Greg Holmes, who shared his playbook on how we can each crack our happiness code.

HEART TO HANDS

A Confession on How
I Fell in the Trap, Hard

ON MARCH 30, 2021, it was launch day for my first-ever book. I poured my heart and soul into every page. My life's work spread from cover to cover.

The anxiety. The tension. The fear. The excitement. The pride. The purpose.

All real feelings and emotions flowing through me when the ribbon was cut.

After months of waiting and internally thinking . . .

- I can't wait!
- What if nobody buys it? What if nobody reads it?
- Dad must be so proud looking over me.
- What if it fails?

I could keep going, but let's just say the process was an emotional roller coaster. Writing the book was actually a pretty smooth process. Launching it was where the bigger lessons were found.

HERE. WE. GO.

It's on Amazon. You refresh sales updates every two seconds. You text everyone you know to spread the word. Your marketing team has their megaphone on full blast.

Then you wait . . . and wait . . . and wait.

The minutes get long. You want everything to happen sooner, better, faster, NOW.

Will it become a bestseller? is all I kept thinking.

You wait . . . you wait . . . you wait.

I made myself some bacon to calm my nerves. Everyone has a guilty pleasure—that's mine. At least I wasn't drinking at 10:00 a.m., but I thought about it!

The day goes . . . and it goes . . . and it goes.

Morning turns to afternoon. What were supposed to be autoupdates every 15 minutes turned into hour-plus gaps between figures repopulating in Amazon and other sales reporting channels. Of course *that's the day* backend technology has glitches.

If you have anxiety reading this, imagine me!

The day turned to night. Still no bestselling news.

I was about to shut it down for the evening, and I hit refresh *one more time.*

The Power of Playing Offense. #1 New Release. #1 Bestseller.

Holy shit!

It happened. I ran to my wife and gave her the biggest bear hug in the world, tears drenching her shoulder. I called mom. My team. My inner circle. We popped some bottles.

Life was AMAZING.

Eventually got some z's.

Then I woke up. Went through my a.m. routine.

And just when I was about to hit my laptop and phone to game plan all the PR and marketing that was to come, I had a weird feeling.

The weirdest part was . . . I had no feeling.

It was like my emotions were numb. I wasn't sad. But I wasn't happy. I wasn't tired. But I wasn't awake. I definitely didn't feel alive.

I thought to myself, *Where the hell is the special feeling that I'm supposed to be feeling right now?*

I just became a bestselling author. Where's the magic? Where's the confetti (in my head or on the ground)? I don't care—I just want confetti!

I'd love to tell you I knew what the problem was in the moment. But I didn't. So I went on with my day and did what was on the calendar. Interviews, social media, some press, and then midday I stopped.

I thought to myself, "You dummy, you never stopped to smell the roses." That's it! That's why I felt like crap on the inside. I forgot to smell the roses! So I had some folks over and more bottles were popped.

Over the coming days I realized it had little to do with smelling the roses.

It had everything to do with falling into the external happiness trap.

I set myself up for failure, and I didn't even know it.

I'll be happy when . . . I become a bestselling author.

The really shameful thing about that statement is, I was at that time—and am today—TRULY a very happy person.

Yet I fell into the trap . . . again. Frankly, as I reflect back, every time I attach some trophy or accolade to happiness, there's rarely a happy ending to the story.

This book roller coaster is one instance.

Another example was my first vice president title. Another time it was a salary bump to a number I set a goal for years prior. Another time it was the typical grass-is-greener job hop. The list goes on. This time it was becoming a bestselling author. Other people said it was a big deal, and I drank the Kool-Aid too hard.

Bravo, Paul. You did it. And what does it even mean?

Two lessons, both linked to better decisions and greater confidence in the future.

1. **Life is a significance game. Not a success game.** Success is serving self. Significance is serving others. When I made it about me, it deflated me, and confused me, as this story illustrates. Success is so momentary, temporary, and at times, hollow. The party ends *real quick*. Had I flipped the script to significance (which I now have) to say, the goal of the book becoming a bestseller is so it can get in the hands of more people and more businesses—leading to greater impact, purpose, and positive influence in people's lives. That mindset and heartset doesn't crash and burn. Chase significance over success. You ALWAYS have a choice.

2. **You've never made it.** Every time you think you have, you haven't. The reality is, the goal posts in life continue to move further and further away. You hit a goal, now you chase the next. You made $5, now you want $10. Every car is an *upgrade* in waiting. Nice house leads to better house. You get it. When we decide to focus on external metrics to bring happiness, we lose. When happiness is centered around green lights of people, relationships, moments, memories, contributions, and experiences that matter, we not only win Monday; we win every day.

PART III

GREEN LIGHTS OF THE HANDS

Taking Purposeful Action

Do you want to know who you are? Don't ask. Act!
Action will delineate and define you.
—Thomas Jefferson

HANDS IS HOW YOU show up. Every decision leads to an action (or inaction).

Consider the head and heart your decision-making drivers and filters.

The hands are the proof that you're actually living it. They make the payouts of action possible.

No need to ask if your head and heart are on board if your hands are unwilling to follow the green lights.

When a green calls, you answer—no matter what.

A good friend and fellow thought leader, Sterling Hawkins, has built an entire movement around the message and spirit of #NoMatterWhat.

His movement rallies people like you and me around the art and science of setting intentions, every day, no matter what.

Whether small or large, Sterling says you should make a decision to do something that brings you closer to your goal every single day—à la Winning Monday, it might be five minutes of intense attention or five hours of focused work. But whatever your goal, you should make some amount of progress greater than zero every day. It builds confidence and courage within yourself, not to mention that it builds momentum toward your most sought-after outcomes.

When I bounced the early concept of *Better Decisions Faster* and the Head + Heart = Hands Equation off Sterling, he had a refreshing and deeply insightful perspective.

"Many of us spend most of our lives in our heads—where the reasons, excuses, and circumstances live. Our approach to life becomes circumstantial and dependent on the world. But when you spend more time in your heart, you step out of reasons and excuses and find the courage to commit to transformation. You get over fear, analysis, and resistance—and begin pursuing your passions."

Spot-on.

This is the perfect segue to the last H of the 3H equation. We've mastered our mindset (head), clarified the authenticity of our heart, now it's time to roll our sleeves up and activate our hands.

The more we connect and align our hands to the green lights of our head and heart, the possibilities and opportunities that life will present to you will be plentiful.

Perhaps you are on your way to making a better decision faster to

- start your own company;
- reconnect with your family;

- dedicate yourself to a cause;
- rebrand yourself professionally;
- pivot into a new industry;
- make an impact in your community; or
- lead a holistic life, knowing you only have one to live.

Regardless of which of these paths or thoughts may resonate most, these lenses are about to be explored in the coming chapters, where we dive deep into the green lights of our hands: **courage, service, excellence**, and **impact**.

By the end of this section, you will learn to

- divorce fear from failure,
- understand that it's *always* bigger than you,
- will yourself to do what others won't, and
- become the difference maker you are destined to be.

Buckle up for the third and final H of *Better Decisions Faster*.

COURAGE

Divorce Fear from Failure

Courage is standing tallest when fear and risk are highest.
—Paul Epstein

THESE WORDS CAME TO me at the darkest possible time.

I had never been more afraid.

Until then, I didn't even fathom the risk that was in front of us—emotionally, financially, or in spirit.

When my dad passed, I walked in the house and saw my mom crying on the ground. I rushed over, picked her up, and she gave me the deepest hug humanly possible.

As I looked into her soaked eyes, I instantly knew life would never be the same.

I had to grow from a boy to a man.

She suddenly shifted from parent to partner.

Failure as a person was no longer an option.

I had to divorce all fears and insecurities.

It was as if the most critical life lessons she had taught me in the first 19 years of my life—lessons that I heard but didn't really listen to—finally sunk in. In this moment of crisis, I found calm knowing that I had her by my side. As we embraced, she breathed courage into me, and it's never left.

Courage is now a core value of mine, and I'm not sure it would be had it not been for losing my dad at a young age.

What convinced me that courage was a nonnegotiable in life was seeing how my mom showed up on the day he passed, and the next day, and the next. She wore the hat of planner, healer, consoler, rock, and leader, all at once. She stood tallest when fear and risk were highest, and I'll never forget it. Her consistent action was life affirming to me.

Mom became a green light when I needed it most.

This chapter is about what is required when life does the opposite of what you want. When life deals you red after red after red. You'll hear stories of misfortune, anguish, radical vulnerability, and a terminal fate. You'll also hear how, paradoxically, triumph, achievement, success, and significance can complement these circumstances—and allow resilient people to overcome them.

From a pair of physically challenged yet unparalleled athletic heroes who made history and set world records against all odds to an unforgettable story of graduating from the prison yard to Harvard Yard—after a life sentence, this chapter has the potential to transform you.

But first you must be courageous enough to step into it.

Against All Odds

Two people. Each on a mission. Against all odds.

Even though one physically can't stand, the other can't see where he's walking, both confidently stand among the tallest titans I know.

Zion Clark was born with a rare birth defect called caudal regression syndrome, which caused him to be born without legs. He was given up for adoption at birth, as his mother was not fit to take care of him. Then he bounced in and out of prison.

Seventeen years of foster care. Nine different homes.

Dealing with relentless abuse—physically, mentally, emotionally—he was taken advantage of and labeled a "problem child" due to his birth defect and lack of parental support.

But then wrestling came into his life, serving as an escape and an outlet. Perfect timing, as he was within six months of aging out of the foster care system and being sent to a group home, when he was adopted by somebody who to this day he calls mom.

Present times, Zion is a world-record holder, elite wheelchair racer, Netflix documentary star (self-named), and is on a quest for Paralympic gold.

Shifting gears . . .

Meet Jake Olson, a fellow Trojan like me. You may know Jake, as he is famously known as the first completely blind NCAA Division I college football player, taking a historic snap as long snapper for USC.

He has since used this experience to inspire and motivate others by speaking and authoring two books, while also creating a nonprofit to help visually impaired children and support cancer research. His story has been featured on ESPN, ABC, NBC, CBS, CNN, Fox, and in the *Wall Street Journal*, the *New York Times*, the *LA Times*, *Sports Illustrated*, the *Washington Post*, and more. Today he's a thriving entrepreneur (cofounder of an explosive talent and experience booking platform Engage) and has a vision to become a pro golfer.

Both joined my podcast to talk about their journeys and courageous decisions along the way.

Here's a quick excerpt from my conversation with Jake, picking up from where he was already blind in one eye since he was an infant:

At the age of 12 years old, cancer came back for its eighth time. Unfortunately, the doctors said, "You have pretty much maxed out on chemo. You've maxed out on radiation. You'll start developing other things if we go down those paths again. The cancer isn't responding to that as strongly as we needed to. There's really no other treatment options we see that would effectively cure this cancer.

So I thought, if we start messing with the eye again, it could spread and take my life. I asked what options there were, only to hear that the only option was to take the eye out. But obviously this was my remaining eye, my only eye I had. That meant permanent blindness for the rest of my life. That was a gut wrenching decision, extremely difficult and tough to make, especially after fighting for 12 years. That's the situation I found myself in the fall of 2009.

If this was your diagnosis, how do you respond?

In Jake's case, the undeniable answer is to compete. This was advice he received from mentors, including former legendary USC football coach Pete Carroll only a few years after this devastating news.

As Jake said: "Competitive environments can change, but the type of competitor you are really matters. You have to always have that staple of knowing who you are. What type of competitor you want to be in those different arenas is what's going to be that difference maker."

Desire to make a difference was the fuel that propelled Jake to keep fighting and beat cancer, by always competing.

Over to Zion . . .

He shared a few insights that led to his personal transformation. For one, opportunity is a matter of perspective. He learned to master and multiply his potential when life tried to subtract his possibilities.

"Part of growing is accepting what life is in that moment, and still pushing forward anyway," he said. "I accepted that my life was crappy, shitty, just not very desirable at all. But at the same time I was like, 'Well, whatever happens happens. I'm just going to keep trying my best every day. To put it simply, *I got sick and tired of being sick and tired.*'"

For both Jake and Zion, life may have taken away some of their physical abilities, but they made the courageous decision to not allow it to take away the spirit of their head, heart, or hands. Both conquered their fears, rebuilt their lives, won a ton of Mondays (and some Saturdays), and reinvented themselves from the inside out.

It's your turn for reinvention, starting by conquering your fears. Courage needs fear, or it will have nothing to overcome.

{🧠} + ♡ = 🙌

DECISION DRILL

Write down your top two fears in life. One personal. One professional.

Personal Fear: _____

Professional Fear: _____

Now it's time to erase barriers. As Jake said, "If something in your control is stopping you, don't let it."

For each of the fears above, what are the barriers (red and yellow lights) you impose on yourself each day, and what is getting in the way of overcoming your fear?

Personal Barrier: _____

_____

Professional Barrier: _____

_____

What green lights can now emerge once you remove these barriers?

Personal greens to look forward to: _____

_____

Professional greens to look forward to: _____

_____

Congrats on facing your fears.

Now marry consistency to courage . . . you'll be unstoppable.

From the Prison Yard to Harvard Yard

One hundred years.

That's a long life.

Now imagine it's a life sentence—to prison.

Andre Norman heard this sentence at 18 years old.

No future. No purpose. No hope.

Today Andre is known to many as the Ambassador of Hope and top global change agent, inspiring countless people to courageously turn their situation around regardless of circumstances.

His work has impacted communities in the Bahamas, Guatemala, Honduras, Liberia, Sweden, and Trinidad. His lectures have reached multiple TEDx stages, London Business School, even Harvard Business School.

You might be asking yourself, *How is this possible? This sounds like the life of two separate people. How do you go from prisoner to professor?*

Kick back, and I'll share some of the backstory and highlights from my one-on-one conversation with Andre.

Andre grew up in a house of domestic violence. By day, his dad sold drugs. By night, he beat Andre's mom.

Add on the racial tension of rocks being thrown at the first school buses he ever got on, a part of the Boston desegregation process, where bused children of color were frequently menaced and attacked, and you can see why Andre had a turbulent start. It only compounded from here.

Dad left the home (and all six kids) when Andre was in first grade. Andre couldn't read.

He was put in special needs class and told it was the "dummy" class.

He somehow got through elementary school only to realize that conditions and kids in middle school were even harsher. They called him stupid, poor . . . the red lights were starting to flash.

So he found people who did accept him.

He started "hustling" in the park. Soon Andre realized he was a part of a gang.

Back at school he starts to play the trumpet and becomes quite good at it. But his gangmates told him that was foolish. So he went back to hustling on the streets.

At 18 years old this lifestyle landed him in court.

"Seven to 10. Nine to 10. Fifteen. Twenty . . ." By the time the judge was through, Andre faced the terminal reality that he would spend his next 100 years of life in prison.

The first thing he did in prison . . .

He joined a gang.

Within years, he was a gang leader. His influence and anger were so hard to control that the system kept bouncing him around from prison to prison, one corner of the US to another.

He became so dangerous that this quickly landed him in solitary confinement.

Six years into solitude, he had an epiphany . . .

He was the king of nowhere.

This realization led to a string of green lights and better decisions—one Monday at a time.

Andre soon started to read. He got a therapist to work through his mental health issues. He checked himself into anger management programs. He started to pursue a GED. Most importantly, he had a goal. "I'm gonna go to Harvard."

When I asked Andre where this belief (and courage) to have such a bold vision during such a dark chapter came from, he credited his therapist in prison.

I asked him to explain.

In a life littered with red lights, Andre said, "I had a lens as a child. These three lessons are how I viewed the world."

Notice how these are all tied to decisions:

1. It's OK to hit people (my dad did it).
2. I'm going to protect myself (like I wanted mom to).
3. I can quit anytime I want (my dad did it). This led to me quitting school programs, sports, music, anything. If dad can do it, I can do it.

"My therapist helped me draw the line between my father walking out and me accepting quitting is a possibility and it's OK," he continued.

"Once we fixed that quitting gene, then my goals of going to Harvard, my goals of going to the moon, all became possible because I was going to go or die trying."

Inspired by his vision, course-correction, and dream, in 1999 Andre won his appeal and walked out of prison after serving 14 years.

This story of resurrection and redemption fueled by better decisions has led to Andre founding the Academy of Hope.

There are lessons we can all pull from Andre's playbook of courage and hope.

For one, don't play the tapes.

Tapes are the messages we tell ourselves that hold us back.

Andre believes we each have a series of tapes (typically yellow or red lights) that play in our heads when we want to pursue something: "You can't do that. You're not capable. You're X, Y, and Z."

But there's no guard at the gate but you. You're the only one stopping yourself from a life of more green lights.

Second, let's engage with your tombstone.

Words of wisdom from Andre: "If you can't line it up on your tombstone, it is just something you picked up along the way. So everything that I'm doing lines up with my tombstone because when it's all said and done, that stone is going to say who you were."

DECISION DRILL

Decide what you want written on your tombstone—because there won't be a lot of space there. Rather than trying to be everything to everyone all of your life, focus on what value you have to bring to this world, what passion you can inspire in others. Let those green lights guide your purpose, and let that purpose guide your actions.

If you're not comfortable with this exercise or thinking about mortality, even better. It takes confidence and courage to put pen to paper and process these thoughts.

What will your tombstone say? _____

_____

_____

_____

Commit to the green lights and better decisions required to make this a reality.

Courage Is a Muscle

Just like any other value in *Better Decisions Faster*, think of courage as a muscle. It can be grown, at times torn through, but most importantly, it is never a finished product. On a scale of 1 to 10, your strength in this value may be a 4, or it may be an 8. Either way, intentional practice, discipline, and commitment to the daily development of your courage muscle are the actions required—just as our new friends, Zion, Jake, and Andre taught us.

TO RECAP COURAGE:

1. **Courage is standing tallest when fear and risk are highest.** You need fear and risk to bring courageous green lights and better decisions to life.

2. **People are redeemable.** Be an ambassador of hope and don't be a red-light victim of your circumstances.

3. *Bonus from mom:* **breathe courage into others.** It can be the best medicine during crisis or tragedy.

Courage is the perfect kickoff to the Hands section within the 3H equation. Nobody said aligning your head, heart, and hands was easy. Neither is courage.

But courage is required to earn the life you want. Courage is required to forge forward through your hands with imperfect action. Courage allows you to divorce fear from failure. Courage is what separates those who make better decisions faster versus those who are paralyzed at every significant fork in the road. The courageous few navigate and conquer the most challenging yellow lights, and they stop running reds.

Our courageous Win Monday Community also attacks more green lights, because we stand for something bigger than ourselves.

For bonus content on Courage, scan the QR code for my personal process on how to make more courageous decisions.

SERVICE

It's Bigger than You

Service to others is the rent you pay for your room here on earth.
—Muhammad Ali

WE GROW UP WITH a vision of going to the highest-ranked school, working for the blue-chip company, earning the accolades, and being lauded for our accomplishments. That's winning. Those are the trophies that matter.

Until you realize they're not. The wins are short-lived. They often lack meaning and substance. You wonder why.

Countless people, including many you trust, have told you service will set you free. The message is that you find yourself and purpose when you serve others. Yet while you're on the hamster wheel described above, you often don't believe it. You think service is for "other" people. If success is serving self, and significance is serving others, you convince yourself success is the ticket.

The reality is, each person finds significance in their own way, at their own time. If you're still on the success train, please read these words with an open head and heart. If you know significance (through service) is the right path but aren't sure how to get there, this chapter will help tremendously.

A second misperception about service is that it has to be tied to a greater worldly philanthropic cause or a civic mission, like being a humanitarian, police officer, firefighter, teacher, or nurse. While it certainly can, and it would be noble, these are far from the requirements or table stakes of service.

I have seen firsthand how these roles in society can lead to massive impact and positivity in the world, with three of my cousins being nurses (and my awesome friends April and Jamie being on a mission to heal our nurses by founding NurseHappy), my uncle being a senior officer in the LAPD, and my mom's next-door neighbor serving as a leader in the LAFD, all of them feel called to do what they do, and get out of bed with service as the green light to their head, heart, and hands.

But that's only one path to green.

This chapter is about making a decision to be a part of something bigger than you. One person can be bigger than you. In some cases, it is the Who under your Why—the Who you dedicate your life to (for example, my Hero's Journey with Dad . . . RIP). In other cases, it is the people you serve professionally (whether a business team, community members, patients, students, the list goes on). In other cases, perhaps it is tied to a worldly cause and there is a mission and vision of a nonprofit in your future. Or it can simply consist of being the best possible parent in the world—and that's enough. You start with family, then build the rest of your life around it.

I am not here to tell you *how* to serve. Most important is that you *do* serve.

The amazingly generous people you'll meet in this chapter include a descendant of the founder of the Peace Corps, who left a purposeful legacy behind as well as someone who emerged from a near-fatal explosion as a boy to go on as a man to inspire millions—all driven by something (or someone) bigger than themselves.

Let's step into their stories of service, better decisions, confidence, and contribution so you can then tap into your own.

Do Well, and Do Good

"My grandfather wrote the original blueprint for the Peace Corps."

The first time I heard these words from Aaron Hurst (talking about his grandfather) on the *Win Monday* podcast, my jaw dropped. It was one of those, "Say what, come again"-type of moments.

He explained how the Peace Corps was birthed from a transformative idea built to amplify impact through contribution. When Aaron's grandfather came out of World War II, he thought a great deal about how to avoid World War III. His epiphany was that if people truly spend time collaborating in service working together to understand each other's culture, then we had a chance of truly building understanding. This idea was the beginning of what became the Peace Corps.

Pretty cool, huh?

Aaron is one of the pioneers of purpose. He has become a friend over the years, which isn't surprising, since I was the former Why Coach of the 49ers. When we met, it was a match made in heaven. He is the founder of Purpose Mindset (whose mission is to inspire the next generation to embrace purpose early in life), the bestselling author of the groundbreaking book *The Purpose Economy*, the recipient of the highest honor available to a University of Michigan alum (Go Blue!), and producer of the annual Purpose Workforce Index.

In between these awesome praises and mission-driven work, he founded the Taproot Foundation, which served as a catalyst for the $15 billion pro bono service market—an organization that was inspired by his grandfather's foundational work at the Peace Corps. Aaron built Taproot as an organization that harnessed the resources of millions of business professionals to build the origin, or taproot, of the nonprofit sector by encouraging professionals to volunteer their skills. This brainstorm led to the creation of hundreds of consulting projects for nonprofit organizations—a true testament to impact at its finest.

Aaron's recent chapter is where we crossed paths—him with Imperative (a purpose assessment and peer coaching platform), me with what was once Purpose Labs, now PurposePoint, aligning on a vision of what work can be when purpose and service are at the center of it.

Imagine this:

You find yourself working in an environment where you're inspired to go in each day. You show up to serve, contribute, and make an impact. You pour your strengths, gifts, talents, and passions into every action you take, and the performance takes care of itself because you're so invested in what you do and why you do it. At the end of a hard-fought day, you feel fulfilled, not exhausted. You're excited to get up and do it again.

That is the working world that we imagine.

A working community that does well *and* does good.

What if this could become a reality for us all?

The gap between current state and this visionary optimal state is what keeps Aaron and me up at night.

To lay the foundation for this vision, Aaron shared some thoughts on how purpose-centered service came to be—surely some of this came from his conversations around a fireplace with his grandfather. Boy, would I have loved to be a fly on that wall.

In the ancient times, before jobs and titles, there was purpose.

Before jobs, managers, and infrastructure, we were all just people working together to survive. But our lives would have been filled with purpose—caring for our tribe, caring for the people around us, and finding ways to stay alive and stay healthy.

So how do we bring that connectedness back to a world where so many things seem to stand in the way?

For starters, Aaron suggests we see people as people.

This perspective is what makes companies do well and do good.

The workforce must be designed for human beings, and if you don't treat your team members and customers as human beings, you're missing an opportunity. Not only are you missing out on creating joy and fulfillment in people's lives, but you're also missing out on the chance to maximize employee engagement, customer loyalty, and shareholder value.

So, for any naysayers of service out there, we should think of purpose and people at the forefront of our Head + Heart = Hands business model.

Every company starts with a purpose. At a point, they invite people to join them on the journey. Process is created. Performance is measured. Profits are achieved.

Purpose.

People.

Process.

Performance.

Profits.

These 5 Ps should be harnessed and harmony should be created among them. When we can effectively do this, the vision of the working world Aaron and I imagine won't be so crazy after all.

In closing, here's a scientific method Aaron taught me on how individual contributions and service can show up at work.

DECISION DRILL

Want to understand how you can serve? Go back to chemistry class.

In science, we learn about forming a hypothesis, testing that hypothesis, and measuring your results. We should do the same in our careers. Run an experiment in which you show up differently, try something new, build a different relationship, or make time to reflect. Build your career as a science experiment and watch what green lights you can learn and discover.

What experiment will you run? _____

_____

What's your first step, and by when? _____

_____

How will you measure your results? _____

_____

Climbing the Right Ladder

BOOM!

Your house blows up.

Not a fairy tale.

This is the tale of John O'Leary, who at nine years old blew up his parents' home and barely survived himself.

NOT a better decision faster!

One hundred percent of his body burned. He was given a 1 percent chance to live.

Google his name to get the full backstory.

Yet here he is. A two-time national bestselling author and world-renowned thought leader who hosts the *Live Inspired* podcast, which has more than 2.5 million downloads and speaks to over 50,000 people every single year.

But it didn't happen overnight. In fact, this gap of impact and service took decades. It wasn't until John realized there was a difference between being awake and feeling alive when John emerged from out of the fire and into the hearts of millions.

He credits countless others, including his mom, teachers, and Jack Buck (legendary voice of the St. Louis Cardinals, father of current Hall of Fame broadcaster Joe Buck), but it was someone else who made the earliest impact on John while the wounds were still fresh.

His dad taught him the power of empathy by showing love and grace through pain and suffering. John shared the details with me on my podcast:

> About an hour and 20 minutes after the explosion, he comes into the room. And I'm sure I'm in trouble. I am burned on my entire body. I burned down his house. I know he's going to be mad. My nine-year-old logic at play. And he walks over to me, and all he says is, "John, look at me when I'm talking to you." And then he added, "I have never been so . . ." and this is a tough type-A alpha dog veteran, "I've never been so proud of anyone in my entire life and never so proud of my little buddy than this morning. I'm just proud to be your dad." And then he says, "I love you. I love you. I love you. And there's nothing you can do about it."

So it's this remarkable story of a little boy who made every wrong decision in the book, burnt himself terribly, burnt down his own mom and dad's house, got whisked off to the emergency room. Doctors begin the treatment. Dad walks in and rather than the expected judgment, just love, man. And so that's such a turning point for me because before he came in, I wanted out.

I mean, some of us listening to my voice have been there or you're there. I wanted out. I'm in pain. I'm looking down and my body's different. I remember what I did at the house. I know what's coming next. I want out. And although he did not take away the pain or the five and a half months to follow, or the two years of surgery and therapy, that grace and that love and that empathy to meet me where I was, was a turning point. Just a transformational turning point in my story, and how we need others.

While it may have taken decades to fully manifest or materialize, the empathy and heart shown by his dad has become a part of John's aura and why he serves to this day.

Maybe there's somebody you need to show empathy toward in this moment?

Dogear this page so you know where you left off, and make it happen. No crisis or tragedy needed for this better, faster decision. A simple phone call or text of empathy will do. Seriously, do it now. I'll wait ...

Welcome back.

Beyond the miraculous story of John's survival, he relayed a story I'll never forget, one of the most profound I've ever heard. I think of it almost daily.

It's about a ladder, and it may just change your entire perspective on life.

From a man who John visited: "If you had visited me about a decade ago, you would've seen a man who was on top of the world. I ran a business. I had no needs whatsoever financially. We were successful. I was married with three kids. Everything was perfect. And in the pursuit of success, I gave into stress and addiction."

The man told John about health issues that followed, decisions he made with alcohol and drugs, and how it cost him financially, then the business, then his marriage, and then his relationship with his kids.

"And then he looked out the window, and it was this painful pause," John said. "He looked back at me and said, 'John, I made it to the very end of my life. *I climbed to the very top rung of that ladder, only to realize I had the damn thing leaned against the wrong wall.*'

"And, dude, when I heard that I was probably 30, but this idea of pursuing something and being so dedicated to it, that you might get to the very top of this thing and recognize the very thing you've climbed was leaning against the wrong wall. I think nothing would be worse than becoming successful at things that just don't matter. At the end of the day, they just don't matter. For me, it was a lesson on pursuing success, but making sure that if the success is true, that it serves something even bigger than myself."

Just like this story hit home with John, it had the same effect on me. Imagine spending your entire life climbing a ladder, only to realize it was a red or yellow light waiting for you at the top—and there's no turning back. There's no next ladder. And the time that you wasted climbing is gone.

That's the power of checking in with your head and heart. It assures you a green light and better decision is what your hands are grasping toward as you climb upward.

It's your turn.

DECISION DRILL

What are the ladders you're climbing in your life? _____

_____

Are you confident you're climbing toward a green light? _____

_____

Is it success (serving self), significance (serving others), or both
that fuel your climb? _____

_____

These answers will define whether your ladder is leaning on a
green wall, a yellow wall, or red wall. Take your time with this
exercise. It can be life-changing.

Choosing the right ladder and the right wall for the right reasons,
in service, can be the best decision you've ever made.

Is Service a Short Game or Long Game?

As we've seen, service comes in many forms.

To answer the question, it's a "yes, and . . ."

Service can be a short AND a long game.

The short game can be serving yourself through daily personal development like reading this book. Actions like that allow you to more effectively serve others. The short game can be showing up as the best parent, friend, employee, or leader possible *today*. It can be committing within the next 30 days to a volunteer effort that would fulfill you. Winning Monday is a weekly reminder of the short game.

Long game starts with vision. Who do you want to serve? Why do you want to serve them? What steps are required to make it happen? And how will you keep going when obstacles arise?

I'll provide a quick peek behind the curtain of my long game of making better decisions as an example.

I want to serve youth. From my dad's legacy as an educator, I see a tremendous amount of purpose in giving back and paying forward what I've learned to the life leaders of tomorrow.

This will involve speaking to educational institutions as much as I do corporate groups, writing books for kids, and teaching students the life lessons and skills that aren't taught in class.

Is everything I just said happening tomorrow? No.

Do I have all the details mapped out? No.

Is it happening? 100 percent. Hell, yes!

Most important is that the vision of serving youth is driving me forward. It gets me through the bad days, drives me to keep fighting when things aren't ideal, and inspires my visioning sessions with my team. It makes me the best possible parent to PJ because I don't want to be a hypocrite when I influence and impact other youthful heads and hearts.

Service can happen daily. *And* it can happen in the future, so long as you commit deeply to it, one day, decision, and action at a time.

1. **Just like businesses can do well AND do good, so can you.** This is why *Better Decisions Faster* is a community. It takes a village to be our best.

2. **Pick the right ladder to climb and lean it against the right wall**. Or you'll find yourself looking back at decades of red and yellow lights, and that wouldn't serve a soul.

What good would service be if we didn't strive to do it with excellence?

For bonus content on Service, scan the QR code to learn how the former head of talent at Chick-fil-A has impacted countless careers, and you can too. P.S.—how good is that spicy chicken sandwich?!

EXCELLENCE

Do What Others Won't

We are what we repeatedly do. Excellence, then, is not an act but a habit.
—Aristotle

WHEN RONNIE LOTT, NFL Hall of Famer and fellow Trojan alum (Fight On!), handed me this football for my mom, it meant the world.

Partly because of what he had accomplished and represented over an illustrious career, partly because I knew how special my mom would feel when receiving it, and partly because of the simple yet profound message.

Be Your Best!

He not only talked about the standard; he decided to BE the standard. On one of the NFL's greatest dynasties, Ronnie was the defender who consistently shut down the other team's best receiver, delivered the bone-crushing hit, and made the game-winning (often game-saving) tackle.

Ronnie did what others wouldn't so he could achieve what others couldn't.

These could just be inspirational words scribbled on a football, but for Ronnie it was how he stepped into each day of his life.

Some of you football fans may know this story, but it's worth repeating. During a game in 1985, Ronnie injured his left pinky while making a tackle. The 49ers went on to win the game and qualify for the playoffs; however, Ronnie's pinky required surgery and eight weeks of recovery. With the playoffs looming, he faced a decision.

Option A.: Surgery = no playoffs.

Option B.: Play through the pain. Doctors disallowed it.

So he went with *Option C* to create his own better decision—and he had to make it fast. Instead of surgery and rehab, Ronnie decided to amputate his pinky. Sure enough, he was out there playing the following week, to be his best for his team.

With any luck, you and I will never have to amputate a finger to achieve excellence. But the decisions on what separates you from the pack will likely require doing what others won't, as there is very little traffic on that extra mile. Those that Win Monday—and in Ronnie's case, Win Sunday—wouldn't want it any other way.

In this chapter, you will hear from brothers who share a message of legendary success (one as a Dallas Cowboys executive, the other as a renowned thought leader) to the modern-day Spartan himself—you may have heard of his endeavor, the Spartan Race. Then a bonus guest: a leader of culture at a $4 billion organization who ALSO coaches mindset performance to a top-ranked college football and NFL team.

It's time to be your best.

Be Legendary

I was sitting in the audience of our global sales conference at Legends, the sports agency I previously mentioned with Greg Kish in chapter 9, owned by the Jones (Cowboys) and Steinbrenner (Yankees) families.

The conference goal was simple: level up our leadership and dominate our sales performance.

The head of Legends global sales at the time: Chad Estis.

Our keynote speaker: Ryan Estis (his brother).

Game on.

Ryan was phenomenal. Beaming with confidence.

Chad and I continued to lock arms in Legends over the coming years. He was one of the big reasons I landed in the NFL league office and headed up revenue for Super Bowl XLVIII.

Years later, after staying in close touch, I had Chad on my podcast.

Now serving as executive vice president of business operations for the Dallas Cowboys, Chad and I were exchanging war stories and banter about our old industry. We had a blast.

I loved how open and vulnerable Chad got, especially for somebody who had since climbed the ranks as an executive in the NBA and NFL. He dove deep on his early struggles, at an entry-level of selling, and how he lacked confidence because of it.

I asked him how he dug out of that hole.

He talked about his prior playing days in college basketball. Chad served as the captain of the 1994 Mid-American Conference Championship team at Ohio University, but before that high mark he had humble beginnings there as well.

When he related his selling struggles to his sports struggles, it clicked.

"If you have nothing else, you can work," Chad said. "If you're not sure of your path, focus on what you do know. I arrived in the world of sales and business and I wasn't quite sure what I was doing in either. But I remembered how I thrived in college hoops—by simply outhustling everyone else."

So he applied that effort to his work—and hustle became a calling card.

He also recognized a conversation he had with his older brother, Ryan, who told Chad that self-education and deciding to invest in yourself is one of the best (and fastest) ways to succeed and persevere through challenges.

Chad referenced a document that he studied constantly in those early days. It was a document that I was very familiar with.

We used it at Legends all the time. It was called the "30 Steps to Success."

30 STEPS TO SUCCESS

1. Effort breeds success	2. Education—get smart!	3. Professional appearance	4. Enthusiasm	5. Product knowledge
6. Training never stops	7. Practice—talkin' bout practice	8. Ask effective questions	9. Sell the benefits	10. Assume the sale
11. Ask for the order	12. Sell past the no	13. Follow-up is critical	14. Handwritten notes	15. Customer service
16. Building relationships	17. Know your competition	18. Know your clients	19. Sell yourself	20. Stick to your word
21. Time management	22. How prepared are you?	23. Goals	24. Teamwork	25. Difficult prospects
26. Mentoring	27. Surround yourself with success	28. Underpromise—over deliver	29. Last call	30. Be fit; take care of yourself

DECISION DRILL

Pick one of the 30 steps you believe in most that you will commit
to: your biggest green light. You don't need to be in sales. Most
are geared for success in life. Some more head focused, others
heart, others hands. No matter what, they're right up our alley.

Your Top Green Light/Step to Success is: _____

_____

Why? _____

_____

I told him how much these 30 steps had inspired me and given a
boost to my career as well, and I gave Legends all the credit for it.

That's when he said it wasn't Legends. It was Ryan. He created it!

I was like, "Dude. No freakin' way." This whole time I thought it was
Legends. We laughed about it as he half-apologized for not previously
giving Ryan the shoutout he deserved.

Most important was that these 30 steps to success created countless
stars in the sports industry and beyond, all because of Ryan's decision
to work on self, which inspired him to share his top learnings, lessons,
and insights with others.

I've recently formed a much closer relationship with Ryan as well, as
he is a top thought leader and speaker in the sales and leadership space.

In seeing one of his past blog posts, *What Does It Take to Be Successful*, these 30 steps to success were included, and it's no shock which one Ryan holds in highest regard.

#1. Effort Breeds Results.

For Chad, effort got him out of an early career funk and propelled him to industry excellence. He's considered by many to be on the Mount Rushmore of sports industry leaders, along with Scott O'Neil (featured in chapter 10) and others.

The parallel in Ryan's story (to Chad's) from his blog is eerie. Check this out.

Subtitle: The Power of Hard Work.

"After nine months at my first sales job, I still hadn't made a sale. That's when Jim Rohn saved me. In one seminar, he set me on fire by sharing information that no school or company was going to provide.

The formula I needed to thrive?

Committing to continuing my education + investing a lot more time in mastering my craft.

Happy hour and softball leagues could wait. I couldn't stomach the idea of getting fired and moving back into my parents' house (that used to be considered failure) to sell baseball cards for beer money. I wanted to succeed. I got to work.

Jim shared timeless wisdom about decisions, discipline and delayed gratification. I was deeply moved. I still have my notes from that night . . .

I put in the 17 years I needed to earn my opportunity. I got really good at something. When you get good at something, nobody can take that from you. The experience matters and it informs my approach to running my own business today."

Legendary BDF perspective and advice. Thank you, Ryan and Chad.

No Retreat: Spartan Up

Our next member of the Win Monday Community needs no introduction, but I'll do it anyway.

Joe De Sena is the founder and CEO of Spartan, the world's leading endurance sports brand. From years trading on Wall Street to a later move to a farm in rural Vermont, which is now his training grounds, Joe turned his passion for adventure races and endurance events into the Spartan Race—one of the most respected adventure events on earth. Now a multiple-time *New York Times* bestselling author and host of CNBC's *No Retreat: Business Bootcamp*, Joe's work has been featured in *Business Insider*, *Men's Health*, *Inc.*, *Forbes*, ESPN, and the *Joe Rogan Experience*.

In true Spartan Race form, we're going to tackle the coming pages a bit differently. Just like a race, there will be a gauntlet of challenges. Or in this case, a gauntlet of Decision Drills. Three, to be exact.

You ready?

Regardless if you are, it's time to Spartan up and get after it!

DECISION DRILL 1

Joe calls this the No Retreat mindset.

Joe has built his life on the idea that we all can go so much further than we think we can. When we begin to feel ourselves getting pushed, we retreat (often staying stuck in a nasty yellow). But what if we took that yellow feeling of discomfort as a sign to push even further? What if we never retreated? Who knows what green lights and better decisions we might persevere to accomplish.

What makes you uncomfortable? Physically, mentally, emotionally? Jot down a handful of examples.

1. _____

2. _____

3. _____

4. _____

5. _____

Now pick one that you're willing to wrestle with and battle through the discomfort.

_____

This is your next yellow light that will soon be a green when you put in the work.

Congratulations—you're through the first round. But no rest for the weary.

DECISION DRILL 2

Want toughness? Practice it.

Toughness is like a muscle.

The science (and Joe) agree—mental toughness isn't something you're simply born with, and it's not generational. Babies born in the 1800s were evolutionarily identical to us today. They survived without the internet, without AC or heat, without the ability to have whatever food they wanted anytime. And yet they survived.

Identify the things in your life that are causing your mental toughness to atrophy, and develop exercises that will help you strengthen it.

What is weakening your mental toughness? What are the self-inflicted red/yellow lights that constantly pull you down? _____

_____

_____

_____

Red/yellow lights block our ability to make better decisions faster. What is an exercise that can help you strengthen your mental toughness and the red/yellow light you identified (mindset shift, a conversation with a coach, a change in your morning routine)?

_____

_____

If this last question stumped you, or you feel there could be a better exercise for you, this is a great opportunity to connect with fellow members of the Win Monday Community to pick their brains. Maybe even share the experience together. Full details on how to access the community are in the book's final pages.

Home stretch. It's time to put a fight on the calendar.

Direct from Joe on my podcast, inspired by legendary boxer Mickey Ward, who said: "What I learned early in life was that I had to always have a fight on my calendar. If I don't have a fight on my calendar, I'm not pushing limits."

DECISION DRILL 3

Mickey told Joe that while he's always in pretty good shape, whenever there's a fight on his calendar it inspires him to take his fitness to a whole other level. These are the grittiest of green lights.

You get to decide. What's the "fight" you can put on your calendar to inspire you to stay resilient, stay tough, and stick to your goals and standards?

Examples include:

- Sign up for a Spartan Race!

- Have that challenging or courageous conversation you've been putting off.

- Do something you said you would *never* do that challenges you physically, mentally, or emotionally.

- Get creative, tenacious, and scrappy. What is the fight you're putting on your calendar? _____

_____

Congratulations. You made it. You're alive. And you're one step closer to being a Spartan . . . as confident as they come.

Just remember: there is no retreat.

Championship Performance

When you hang with the author who wrote the playbook for building championship mindsets, *Winning the Mental Game*, you know you're surrounding yourself with the right people. In my case, I have the privilege of knowing someone who has coached mindset performance to the Notre Dame football team and is now a mindset coach at LSU on Saturdays, the same for the Denver Broncos on Sundays ON TOP OF serving as head of culture for a $4 billion organization at Lippert. She's also founded her own performance group to instill this championship mindset in others.

Meet Dr. Amber Selking. I'm honored to call her a friend and peer in the space as well as a guest on the *Win Monday* podcast.

Aside from awe and intrigue of her credentials, you may be thinking, *I thought this section was about our hands.* She focuses more on mindset. Fair callout, and this is the perfect time to realign us and say, "They're inextricably linked."

Without a championship mindset, you can't make better decisions faster; there will never be sustained championship performance. It's that simple.

A few keys to cultivating our championship mindset from Amber:

- *Grace.* For too many people, a championship mindset means a relentless, unforgiving slog toward success where any failure, misstep, or decision gone south is unacceptable. But true champions know that sometimes things won't go their way, they don't let their confidence become derailed by these failures, and will give themselves grace to move forward—no matter what.

- *Confidence.* Make your confidence independent of circumstances; confidence is a choice. It doesn't come from achievement; it comes from knowing what you're capable of. For some, that knowledge is bolstered by their achievements. But you don't have to have already found your success to have confidence—just ask athletes who have missed every shot in a game but still have the guts to take that game-winner.

- *Joy.* Don't simply chase goals. Feel joy while getting the results you seek. When you can align your pursuit of both those external goals with your internal goals, confidence grows and you'll find a championship mindset.

TO RECAP EXCELLENCE:

1. **Be Legendary.** Commit to your top BDF step to success (we gave you 30 options!). Literally dozens of possibilities to level up any of the three Hs.

2. **Put a fight on your calendar.** When Joe De Sena challenges you to "Spartan Up," you don't retreat. He squeezes reds into greens as a hobby.

3. *Bonus from Dr. Amber Selking*: **confidence is critical for a championship mindset and performance**. The good news: confidence is a choice. Just like Winning Monday is.

As we round the bases toward home, excellence will lead to making the biggest impact possible. And isn't that what we're here for?

For bonus content on Excellence, scan the QR code to learn how to turn your Fs into As through a holistic life model taught by a lifestyle coach with a waiting list you couldn't fathom. You just cut the line.

IMPACT

Be a Difference Maker

Some people want it to happen, some wish it would happen, others make it happen. —Michael Jordan

EVERY CHAPTER IN THIS book led to this final green light: **impact**.

Impact is the scoreboard that counts. This is why we take action. This is the payout of getting your head and heart aligned to set your hands in motion. This is the end game of making better decisions faster and moving forward with unshakable confidence. Otherwise, this entire book was a fun exercise. It needs to be more. It must mean more.

Impact is why you must **grow**, be **positive**, **gritty**, **curious**, **passionate**, **authentic**, **grateful**, **happy**, **courageous**, and ready to **serve**—with **excellence**.

All green lights within *Better Decisions Faster* represent how you can make a difference, one day, decision, and action at a time.

Warning: Many people get lost when they hear the word *impact*. It sounds too abstract. It lacks clarity.

That's one way of looking at it.

The other is to use its general feel or vagueness to your advantage. Impact is flexible and versatile. Think of impact as the Swiss Army knife of making a difference.

Only you know the difference you are inspired to make. Only you know why you choose to Win Monday.

As impact is a core value of mine, here are a few rules I've always followed:

- **Make a difference that matters DEEPLY to you.** Otherwise, it's too easy to quit when it gets hard. Impact is the dopamine hit that keeps you going.
- **When you make a difference within yourself, others benefit.** Impact is not a scarcity game; it's an abundance game.
- **Make sure your impact aligns with how you want to be remembered.** The more your impact connects to your legacy, the greater the contribution and significance.

Now it's your turn.

To be the difference maker you are meant to be, you'll meet some amazing difference makers in their own right. We start with a friend and founder whose mission is to reveal the heroes of tomorrow. Then we go for gold alongside a Team USA Paralympian player turned coach to hear his golden tale of tragedy to triumph. Bonus round post-chapter, you'll meet my partner at PurposePoint, who gets out of bed to drive impact in all he does, from the boardroom to the classroom to the dinner table and beyond.

He texts me nearly every day: Let's gooooooooooo (I may have cut some Os).

With that, let's go!

Reveal Tomorrow's Heroes

Syed Mohammed is a wonderful human being.

He reminded me of a proverb that he has up on his office wall, a saying that embodies impact at its finest: "The grass is greener where you water it."

Want to make a difference? Start watering there.

I met Syed as he was then the CEO and founder of Enable My Child. Through our partnership, the company is now called Hello-Hero, a collection of courageous providers collaborating to increase access to quality care for children who are in extremely challenging circumstances.

The opportunity for impact is massive, and that's what drew me to Syed, his team, and their mission.

What I love most about Syed is how he leads. He's too humble to call himself a great leader, so I will. There are two attributes that struck me immediately about him.

One, his vulnerability to lead from the front. Two, his focus on impact through his commitment to values (as you'll read shortly).

What does it mean to lead from the front? It's going first and understanding that at times leadership will challenge you to get personal. So you make it personal. I don't just mean vulnerably sharing the skeletons in the closet with your team. I mean caring about what you do so deeply and making it so personally meaningful to you that compassion pours out of you. Everyone sees it, feels it, and is impacted by it.

With Syed, in one of our first conversations, he opened up to me just as he does publicly. He's lived through his own developmental and mental challenges. He was one of the kids who needed special attention as a child. He had an inner hero inside of him who yearned to be unveiled to the world. Decades later, he's solving for the problem (and opportunity) that he once had.

By leading from the front, he has inspired countless others to join him on his journey of turning reds and yellows into life-impacting greens. This includes his team that he cares for unconditionally (I've seen it privately and in tough moments), as well as his external team of school administrators, teachers, families, insurance providers, and children. You cannot reveal the heroes of tomorrow without each and every one of these people doing their part and deciding to contribute their own special impact. Syed knows the collective superpowers of all these people is what allows HelloHero to thrive.

At a workshop I facilitated, Syed and team identified their organization's why: "To reveal tomorrow's heroes." Little did I know that inspiration would also lead to a change in Enable My Child's name to, of course, HelloHero.

SO AWESOME!

We then drilled into the values (a.k.a. green lights) of the organization, much like I'm encouraging you to do in this book. If the goal of aligning your head, heart, and hands is to make better decisions faster so you can drive more impact, values are the fuel for that daily grind and commitment.

For HelloHero, you'll see this on their website:

At HelloHero we live by our values

We do this by staying true to our core values every day with every person we touch. You will see every team member at HelloHero embodying:

- Care
- Collaboration
- Trust
- Courage
- Impact

Through our commitment to these values, we will not only enable more children; we will reveal the true HERO inside them.

This is the value of values.

I'm proud, honored, and inspired to have been a small part of HelloHero's green lights and better decisions to date.

Thank you, Syed and team, for all you do and who you are.

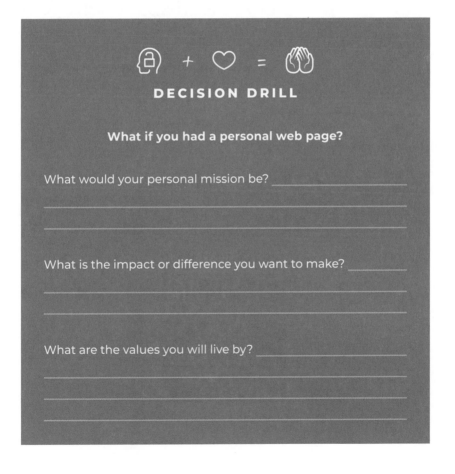

DECISION DRILL

What if you had a personal web page?

What would your personal mission be? _____
_____
_____

What is the impact or difference you want to make? _____
_____
_____

What are the values you will live by? _____
_____
_____
_____

That's a lot; I know. But these are the questions you must face and own when you join the Win Monday Community and embrace the green-light lifestyle.

For all the overachievers out there, you may already be done with your notes.

For the rest of us, I have a resource that can help you ideate your personal mission, values, and beyond.

Since we're talking heroes in this section, what do all heroes have in common? Superpowers. The question is, what are your superpowers? I have a **Superpower Assessment** just for you.

You can either scan the QR code below or it's on pages 196–197 of *The Power of Playing Offense*, if you already have a copy or want to pick one up.

Go reveal the hero inside you!

The Power of Choice

"In that split second, life changed. I go from the boat to the rescue boat to the ambulance to the local hospital. They med-flight me up to a bigger hospital. And that's when I learned that I had a spinal cord injury, that I had broken my neck, and that I'd probably never walk again."

Put yourself in this scenario.

What choice do you have? What decision can you make? The cards have been dealt. Boat struck the bottom of the river. You fly backward, breaking your neck at vertebrae C6 and C7.

You will NEVER walk again.

The rest of life feels like a storm of red. If you're lucky, yellow. Greens are long gone.

Take a moment to absorb that.

This is the exact state Joe Delagrave found himself in, as he described on my podcast. After a casual boating accident that would have derailed most people's lives and shattered their dreams, Joe shared his story through a renewed lens of purpose and transformation.

The key to it all: an undying sense of courage that allowed him to rise above his initial feelings of frustration and depression into a world of confidence, better decisions, and impact.

Joe is now a paralympic athlete for Team USA. That journey doesn't happen without the boating accident, which later introduced him to the sport of wheelchair rugby.

As I talked to Joe about his accident with tears in my eyes, my heart felt wounded for him. But Joe had a shockingly refreshing perspective on what transpired.

He kept coming back to the critical juncture in the road of life when all our hopes and dreams are rejected. We may have had many rejections before (he certainly did prior to his accident), but when we perceive the worst of red lights to be happening . . . we *still* have a choice: Give in and accept the status quo. Or insist that our potential to get back to green is greater than any setback or life circumstance.

Even writing this, Joe's story is difficult to comprehend. I found myself asking how I would have responded to this.

I ask you: *How would you respond?*

How you respond is a *decision.*

When hearing from Joe that we *always* have a choice on how we respond, it shook me. Then, strangely, it grounded me. It reframed how I understood the connection of courage to impact (as I hope it will for you too).

During our conversation, I probed on the "how" of Joe's transformation.

He shared a key shift in mindset that changed his life.

A red to green shift from "*How do I get out*" to "*How do I excel where I am?*"

At first Joe wanted only one thing—to get out of his wheelchair. He felt that was the only way his life could begin again.

Then he pivoted by realizing there are avenues for success while living with disability. That's what initially ignited his curiosity about wheelchair rugby. An athlete for most of his life, one day he was exposed to, in his words, grown men who were beating the crap out of each other with their metal chairs. He thought it looked interesting. He excitedly leaned in. Years later, he went on to thrive at it. He's now represented Team USA at three Olympic Games as a proud Paralympian—an honor only available by him choosing to clearly live and lead with his head, heart, and hands.

How can we all learn from Joe's playbook?

It comes back to the power of choice. Joe's story of personal conquest is a phenomenal reminder that even when you feel your agency is taken away, you *always* have a choice. It's fitting for our Win Monday

Community that ownership of life (the good AND bad) is one of our table stakes.

Joe could have turned to blame, bitterness, indecisiveness, and a feeling of helplessness. Instead, he reminded (along with the help of his inner circle) himself to remember that you always have a choice in how you respond to tragedy or roadblocks. If you can break free from blame (as he initially did toward the boat driver, his good friend), you can find incredible growth and impact on the other side.

DECISION DRILL

While likely less dramatic or extreme than Joe, think of an experience when a life circumstance unexpectedly struck. Something that was completely out of your control, when you initially fell into a deep place of blame toward another person or your surroundings. Likely a painful red light in the rearview mirror. Jot the "when" and "where" below.

Notes: _____

_____

Now ask yourself, have you decided to fully release the blame or are you still living with it? (yes or no)

(yes = fully released; no = still festering) _____

Until we release the blame, we're never fully healed, yellows and reds will not become greens, we're stalled from making better decisions, and we can't move forward. Just like Joe was only able to move on and grow from his horrific circumstance when he released blame from his friend, the boat driver, perhaps now is a good time to shed this heavy weight in your head and heart, to push forward and take the courageous step of owning your life, knowing you always have a choice—not of what happens to you—but how you respond to it.

One final detail about Joe: When we last spoke, he was just named the interim head coach for USA Wheelchair Rugby. Thank you for your continued service and impact, Joe. You're an inspiration to us all. Now go get that gold!

Impact Gets Personal

To all the impact champions out there, keep doing what you do and being who you are. You make a difference. One day. One decision. One action. One person. One mission. One purpose. One contribution. One legacy. One life at a time.

Starting with your own. Then for others. Keep your cup full, so we can continue to pour into others. Cheers to the impact and difference-making still to come, my friends.

TO RECAP IMPACT:

1. **Reveal your inner hero and let your superpowers shine.**
   They are your impact-driven gift to the world. They ignite the *better* in your better decisions faster.

2. **You always have the power of choice.** Decide to drive impact in all you do, regardless of circumstances, because somebody is always counting on you.

We're at the end of our third and final H—Hands. Green lights are dialed in . . .

Courage ☑   Excellence ☑
Service ☑   Impact ☑

Final turn as we enter the home stretch of *Better Decisions Faster*.

Home-stretch highlights include:
- Leading through the Yellow Lights (Conclusion to a Hero's Journey)
- Your Most Valuable Decision—Revisited
- Book Summary: The 11 Must-Knows (and Must-Dos) of *Better Decisions Faster*
- #WinMonday Community: Resources and Action Items

But first, before we do, we must be.

HANDS TO
HOME STRETCH

Be before You Do

MY BUSINESS PARTNER, Davin Salvagno, leads self, leads others, and creates impact at a mastery level. These three leadership layers are the ethos of Davin and PurposePoint's flagship event, the Purpose Summit (from which the Win Monday spirit was inspired).

He learned the impact of leadership through his earliest leadership roles at Costco, Macy's, and CVS Health. Now he is the proud author of *Finding Purpose at Work* and his upcoming release, titled *The Thief of Purpose.*

Ask him what his purpose is, and he'll say purpose comes in many forms. By day, his purpose is to be an encouraging leader at Purpose-Point, which he cofounded and is CEO of. He also has purpose as a teacher, inspiring the leaders of tomorrow at an outer Detroit high school. By night, weekends, and beyond, his purpose is to be a husband and father.

There's a reason I consider Davin more than a partner. For all the purposes and hats he wears, I consider him a kindred spirit and BDF brother from another mother. His head, heart, and hands are FULLY aligned. He wins more Mondays than I can count.

Given my title at PurposePoint is Chief Impact Officer, I asked Davin to define what **impact** means to him.

"Impact is when your life in some way, shape, or form enters the life of another in an indelible way."

Indelible means your impact cannot be expunged. It cannot be erased. When thought of this way, impact takes on a massive sense of responsibility.

My spin on indelible impact is similar and simple: *How are you leaving others better than you found them?*

That is a decision we should all be proud to make.

In order to leave others better than we found them, we must have the same responsibility for ourselves.

How can you leave each day better than you entered it?

Because if your cup is not full of energy, belief, confidence, better decisions, and a spirit of growth, it will be very difficult to pour these qualities into others.

What is Davin's advice on how to best lead yourself so you can then go on to lead others and lead impact?

Be before you do.

Leaders start with who they are—not what they want to do.

Yes, we just concluded the third H (Hands), which is all about taking action (doing), but what is the intention underneath the actions you are taking?

Are they synced with who you want to be?

In other words, are your hands FULLY aligned and sourced from your head and your heart?

That is what Davin is reminding us to do. *Better Decisions Faster* reinforces the process around "being before you do."

Notice we didn't start with Hands. It is the closing act . . . with intention.

One more time. Hands . . . is the closing act . . . with intention.

Still not convinced about *being* before you *do*?

Davin has a perspective that may help. When he speaks about leaders in a professional setting, he says, "Before making requests and moving resources, they must first live their purpose, embrace their gifts and talents, and find their Why. Without that, they're just managers—not true leaders of others or even themselves."

Boom.

Read that quote again and ask yourself: *Am I managing my life?*

Or am I leading it?

You don't *manage* impact. You *lead* impact.

This message is to reorient us on how critical it is to find opportunities for impact around every corner of life. We talk about work here because we spend so much time doing it. If we can solve for that 100,000-plus-hour pool of time in our life, the rest of the dominoes are more likely to fall into place elsewhere. Your potential for impact is limitless, but when you drive impact at work, it's much easier to create impact in life.

Per Davin, "If each of us could see the difference and the impact we make every single day through the work that we—not *have* to do, but the work that we *get* to do—then we would never work a day in our life."

Impact is the scoreboard that counts.

To the home stretch we go.

HOME STRETCH

Your Path to Win Monday

YOU MADE IT. So freakin' pumped for you!

In this book, you're pages away from completion.

In life, you have far to go.

That's the exciting part.

It's time to crystalize what your plan will be to Win Monday—and beyond. This is the point of transformation you've long awaited, sought after, and are now moments from achieving.

I'll be right alongside you as we build a green-light lifestyle, with reds in the rearview mirror and, of course, we conquer the yellow.

That's where we start our home stretch.

- You'll hear the **conclusion of my opening Hero's Journey,** where I faced down the barrel of the most difficult yellow in my life.
- From there, we'll close the loop on **your #1 MVD.**
- Then arm you with the **top 11 takeaways of Better Decisions Faster**—consider this your "go-to" book summary.
- Finally, all details on how to maximize engagement and value from our **#WinMonday Community—action plan and tool kit locked and loaded.**

The impact of these closing pages can match (maybe exceed) the entire read up to this point, if you *decide* to allow it to.

Leading through the Yellow Lights (Conclusion to a Hero's Journey)

I opened this book by writing about one of the toughest periods of my life. From this darkness, I said that I used the Head + Heart = Hands Equation to change my life by making a better decision faster.

That's true . . . but it wasn't easy.

I was six months into fatherhood, and I felt like I was failing the most important test (and yellow light) of my life.

While green lights (head and heart on board) are what we're all after—and trust me, it's pretty sweet—the reality is much of life lies in the nasty middle of yellow. Reds (like greens) are primarily an awareness game. Once you're aware, you seize the green and avoid the red. Yellows, on the other hand, will test you.

My dad was my hero, and I felt like the furthest thing from a hero, wondering how I would get through this storm.

Often times, yellow lights feel like an internal storm.

The storm is the tension.

The storm is the stress.

The storm is the anxiety.

The storm rarely has easy answers.

There is no clear cut solve . . .

Until now.

At the time, I had yet to develop the formula: Head + Heart = Hands.

I didn't refer to life decisions and actions as green, yellow, or red lights.

But in the world of deep inward reflection, personal growth, and identity, answers come to us in mysterious ways, when we lean into it.

I knew my heart was on board. Of course, I wanted to be an awesome dad to PJ. Of course, I wanted to feel like a hero. Of course, I wanted to make my dad in heaven proud of me.

It was my head that kept blocking this harmony.

My head kept thinking of what life was prefatherhood. The joy and freedom of exotic trips, sporting events, and spontaneous date nights with my best friend. The ability to go wherever, hang out with whomever, whenever we pleased. In reflection, all my energy was focused on what I perceived to have lost instead of what I had gained, and it only got worse as time went by.

It wasn't just the experiences "lost"; it was also a gap in identity.

The sleepless nights are where I really questioned the bigger picture. Waking up every two hours to a cry, longing for peace, wanting to help physically and emotionally as a dad and partner (from feeding to support) and yet I felt helpless, like there was little I was able to contribute. No worth. No value.

The moments felt long, and they felt permanent.

Questioning, *Will life ever be the same? Will I ever be the same? Will we ever be the same?*

I knew something had to change.

Within this darkness and sense of desperation, I decided to take a page from my own playbook. So far, I was playing small, and I felt small (**head**).

So I decided to play big (**heart**).

My heart knew that courage was needed.

I decided to confront my yellow head-on, with unshakable confidence, and get off the sidelines (**hands**).

I was done hiding. I was done being embarrassed. I was done being ashamed of not loving being a dad.

My heart led me to take the first step.

I talked to my best friend—my wife, Mayra.

I told her, as raw and real as possible, what I was going through.

Frankly, I was worried she would judge me, question my love for our child, maybe even question our marriage. These are the thoughts that were going through my head.

A reminder that the mind can be a tricky beast, when we conceal our thoughts inside it.

Mayra absorbed everything I said, and in a matter of seconds responded, "I've been waiting for this [conversation] for months. I've seen you every day. You haven't been you. You look sad, and I know that's not you."

No guilt trip. No shame. No judgment.

Then she asked, "Have you talked to your (guy) friends about this?"

I hadn't.

But this was my green light to do so.

Let's not gloss over the fact that I fell in love with Mayra one million times more intensely after this conversation. While she could have yelled, kicked, screamed, and questioned my character—all understandable in the heated moment—she did the exact opposite. Her reaction reinforced that she'd always been the biggest green light in my life.

I went on to talk to my buddies, and it helped . . . a lot.

Within weeks of these conversations, my yellow softened and faded. Days became warmer. The sun became brighter. My insides felt healed. My heart was pumping faster. My head felt uncluttered. I felt free again, like before I was a dad.

But now I was free—as a dad.

I looked into PJ's eyes with a new appreciation. A new love. A new connection.

My *heart* always wanted to be his hero. Now my *head* joined my heart for the party. My *hands* were following with action and belief that this was the biggest blessing of my life.

And I had to go through one hell of a storm to realize this!

This experience taught me everything I need to know (and now you will too) about yellow lights.

They suck and they're hard. So please don't try to tackle them alone (especially the big ones). When you include others, you'll often find they can be heroes in their own right.

Also, where the gap lies (head or heart) is critically important.

In this case, my heart was on board. I needed others to help me battle through the head gap.

I'm afraid that if the opposite was the case, and my heart wasn't on board (even if my head thought it wanted to be), this story doesn't have a happy ending. No hero emerges at the end. No green lights await.

Your heart doesn't change in days, weeks, months. We're lying to ourselves if we think it does, or it will.

So be real.

A yellow head gap can be solved.

A yellow heart gap—and staying in it—is just as deadly as a red.

There's only one path to green, and that is to be aware, be courageous, and overcome the yellows that you can. Some you'll have to let go and move on. That's a massive reason why this playbook was written, so that we could all lead through the complicated and complex yellows, together, as a Win Monday Community. More on this in the book summary to come.

The Head + Heart = Hands Equation can—and will—be a green light in and of itself. It doesn't promise you a green-light outcome; it provides you a green-light process—of clarity, confidence, conviction, and courage, to know that you consistently make the best call, *faster*. Sometimes it's a red light you need to exit immediately, and sometimes it's a solvable yellow (like mine—when you lead from the heart). Sometimes it's a yellow to put behind you, and other times it's an inspiring green to embrace and seek more of. This is what the equation delivers.

I had to walk through mud to inspire it, create it, and now share it, and it was worth every step of the journey.

To PJ and Mayra, I love you.

Thank you for reminding me that every day is a green light to be grateful for, and you (now together) are the biggest green lights of my life.

YOUR MOST
VALUABLE DECISION
—REVISITED

IN TELLING MY STORY at the start of the book, I not only said that the Head + Heart = Hands Equation helped me make a better decision faster—I also said that I believed it could do the same for you. Let's put my words to the test.

In Chapter 1 (page 16) you filled out your MVD. Refer back to refresh your memory, otherwise we'll enter this exercise from scratch. Flip the page—the solution to your MVD awaits.

Write down your most valuable decision.

MVD _____

I promised you that by the end of this book you would be able to attach a green, yellow, or red light to this decision and know exactly what your next move should be.

NOW is that time.

The 3H process is simple, and by this point you should have internalized it, practiced it, and are ready to apply it to life . . . 365.

You know the questions . . . for each decision:

Is your head on board?

Is your heart on board?

If yes to both, green light. Hands confidently take action.

If one is on board, the other isn't, yellow light. Write down which isn't on board as well (i.e., yellow light—head gap, or yellow light—heart gap).

If neither is on board, red light. No action.

MVD (rewrite from above): _____

For your MVD, fill out *Green*, *Yellow—Head Gap*, *Yellow—Heart Gap*, or *Red.*

This color is your next move. You know what to do.

Green. Ignite action!

Red. DON'T take action.

Yellow—head gap. Leverage your #WinMonday Community. Details at the end of the book.

Yellow—heart gap. Just as deadly as a red. A hard (but authentic) decision awaits. Make it better and faster.

To download a worksheet so you can fill out ALL your MVDs, scan the QR code below. We'll provide space for each holistic area of your life that is most valuable to you. My recommendation is to print it and keep it visible in your daily sight so they stay top of mind.

BOOK SUMMARY

The 11 Must-Knows (and Must-Dos) of Better Decisions Faster

Note: all must-knows and must-dos apply personally and professionally—to individuals, teams, and companies alike.

Life is a decision and action game. It starts by Winning Monday. The goal of this book was to simplify a complex world with complex decisions by providing a simple equation to make your most valuable decisions (MVDs) better and faster. Life can be simplified and distilled down to the simple truth that it is a decision and action game. Audit your past to verify.

In business, decisions aplenty, concerning career choices, strategies, deals, hiring, firing, partners, investments, and on and on. These decisions (for better or worse) effect your career, company, success, fulfillment, and income. In life, decisions around relationships, health, money, friends, parenting, time, attitude, priorities . . . it never stops.

Show me quality decisions in these areas, and I'll show you a quality life of happiness, purpose, confidence, gratitude, and significance.

With decisions having such high consequences on what matters most in life, why would you leave it to chance?

The Head + Heart = Hands Equation is your solve to making better decisions faster. It starts Monday. Buckle up and prepare to win.

Better and faster decisions isn't accidental; it's a process.
Welcome in the Head + Heart = Hands Equation. Let's break
down why the Head + Heart = Hands Equation leads to better decisions faster. We all have a natural lean toward head or heart. Logical
and analytical people lean head. Emotion and gut-driven people lean
heart. Without picking a side (usually a bias to what we already are),
they both matter.

Head ensures you *think* it's a good idea. Heart ensures you *feel* it's a
good idea. Again, they both matter. It's not Head or Heart = Hands.
It's Head + Heart = Hands. This 1-2 punch guarantees you're making
the best possible decision in a balanced, sustainable, and repeatable
way. That covers *better*—on to *faster*.

Often within seconds, by using the Head + Heart = Hands Equation, you get to a green, yellow, or red light on your most valuable
decisions. That's not only awesome; it's fast! Seconds (maybe minutes)
fast for what previously would have been a paralyzing fork in the road.
Bottom line: you win time back to reinvest into your family, business,
health—all massive wins in our book.

The cherry on top: hands are the back end of the equation. You
check in with your head, check in with your heart, then decide what
to do with your hands. Nearly instantly, you know whether to take
action or not.

Just remember: Taking action is a decision in and of itself. Commit
to better decisions faster, and it will require you to take action.

The worst decision is indecision. Better decisions faster solves for decision fatigue, overwhelm, paralysis by analysis, and the worst-case scenario, indecision. Making a decision is a decision.

When you sit on the sidelines waiting for the shiny opportunity, hopeful sign, comfortable road free of risk, bulletproof plan, or a perfect time, they never arrive. "Perfect time" is a fallacy. The optimal time is as soon as you reach that green, yellow, or red light. This signal dictates your next move, better and faster.

Green and red are quick triggers (you'll instantly sense both). Yellow requires work. Just don't stay paralyzed in the yellow; it will suck the life out of life. Those who are decisive earn the transformation of going from *living* to *feeling alive* because they take control of their future. The decisive separate themselves from the pack because they are willing to take action in imperfect scenarios, conditions, or seasons.

You can decide to play defense and wait, or you can play offense and win. Just make a call.

4

Awareness, Ownership, and Intention are the table stakes to Win Monday. Much like a poker game has ante to play, so does Winning Monday.

Without *awareness*, you'll never know when to use the Head + Heart = Hands Equation. Opportunities and greens will fly right by you, and blind spots (reds) will surround your every move and decision, or lack thereof. Awareness is also key as it colors how you show up with your mindset, energy, and attitude (more on this in a bit).

Ownership is required as there are no victim mentalities allowed in the Win Monday Community. You own the good AND the bad. Setbacks, hurdles, obstacles, adversity—it's all part of the game of life. Bad and unfortunate things will happen. We own it, we learn from it, we embrace it, we evolve, we move forward . . . better and faster. Own it, no matter what.

Intention is the spirit to step into each day with. People who live by the Win Monday principles don't live life defensively, by accident, or by default. They step into each day with purpose . . . on purpose.

Adopt these three tables stakes of awareness, ownership, and intention, and you will be primed to make better decisions faster consistently, habitually, and for the long haul.

Courage is required for better decisions faster, but clarity and confidence are the START HERE button. Courage is to stand tallest when fear and risk are highest. Even reading those words, you lose some people. Why? We are trained, molded, and wired to avoid fear, risk, and pain. Even though many of us know growth only happens on the other side of discomfort (often filled with inconvenience, risk, fear, the whole nine).

But this formula doesn't merely serve the currently courageous, it infuses and inspires the courageous of tomorrow. Here's how. There are 4 Cs, and they each build onto each other.

The Head + Heart = Hands Equation is designed to provide you Clarity. Once we see clearly, we build confidence. Over time, consistent confidence breeds conviction. Those who are convicted step into a zone of courage.

Clarity → Confidence → Conviction → Courage.

All are required to make better decisions faster—but we must start by knowing who we are (clarity) and leveling up our confidence in order to make these decisions. Inside *Better Decisions Faster*, you have two tools that can help with this—a **WHY discovery** and **Confidence Quiz**, both of which can be accessed through the QR codes below.

WHY DISCOVERY   CONFIDENCE QUIZ

Greens and Reds: Eyes wide open. Be Aware. Be VERY Aware. With greens, when your head and heart are on board, you take action as if nothing else in the world mattered. You attack green lights. You live for the green lights. It's the healthiest addiction you could ever have. A green-light life is priceless. Once you taste one, now that you're aware, you'll never go back to the old way.

Red lights also require awareness. Most of us have been running red lights for years without even knowing it. Subconsciously we have been doing things with neither our head nor our heart on board. Why? Because we didn't have a process . . . until now. The Head + Heart = Hands Equation is your process to STOP running red lights.

When you're feeling off, your gut is giving you signals, your head is tripping you up, your heart isn't feeling warm about something, or you're staring at a fork in the road for a decision that matters—any and all of those are great awareness cues to STOP, check in with your head, check in with your heart, and if neither is on board . . . red light. Abort mission. Get out. Don't take action toward future reds. For current reds, remove them from your life.

Because you're now aware, you can seize the greens and stop running reds.

Not all yellows are created equal + the avoidable death blow.
A yellow naturally means either your head or heart is not on board. But not all yellows are created equal. There is a very different tactical plan on how to address each, and also a common outcome for each—one being a MASSIVE warning sign that could lead to harsh long-term consequences.

Starting with a head gap, don't go at it alone. As you read in my Hero's Journey, often a head gap is simply getting out of our own head. Talk to somebody you know and trust: partner, best friend, coach, parent, mentor. We're likely overthinking something or have a self-limiting belief, or perhaps it isn't the right logical decision and we just need to verify that externally.

Heart gaps, on the other hand, don't have as clear cut of a solution, or process. Simply put, heart gaps are a direct test in your face of how bold and honest you're willing to be with yourself. This is the ultimate authenticity test. Your heart doesn't change overnight like your mind can. Your heart is largely set. It knows what it feels. The question is whether you accept that reality. Is this the person, job, or life you REALLY want? Only you know that. Your heart knows that.

So, when your heart is not on board (a heart gap), it's up to you to make the hard call and remove that yellow from your life. Because if you don't, you may find yourself, 12, 24, 36 months later wondering how you got there. Bad relationship, miserable career, lost in life. It's likely a heart gap yellow where your mind convinced you to stick with it (for the security, paycheck, fear of change), and now you're in an eternal yellow, until you decide to not let it be that way.

A long-term yellow is just as deadly as a red.

Lead from the heart. It's a forgotten art. The world is largely wired to think with their head and act with their hands. I don't need to convince people to think more, or do more. Where the gap lies is in between.

Who are we being? When do we pause, call a timeout, reflect with intention, audit our past to better understand our present and cast a vision for our future? Words like purpose, significance, joy, fulfillment, mission, and impact don't need to feel so farfetched or out of reach. Through the heart, they're all at our fingertips RIGHT NOW.

Our entire lives we've been told to make **smart decisions**, when it turns out our best decisions are often **heart decisions**.

Do I believe ONLY focusing on your heart is the right strategy? No. That's why it's not the Heart Equation. We've largely already got the head and hands boxes checked. This newfound equation ensures we don't skip over the heart. It provides balance to think *and* feel, logic *and* emotion. Most important, it guarantees authenticity. Your heart is the authenticity driver of the Head + Heart = Hands Equation. If you lead from your heart, you'll make better decisions faster.

At the next fork in the road you face, start by checking in with your heart. If it's on board, you're either on a path to a green or yellow (to then solve the head gap). Either way, these are the two best lights you could possibly have, because you're leading with your heart—and that, my friend, is a forgotten art.

Not all decisions are forks in the road; you have MVDs every day. When we think of Most Valuable Decisions, we think of the bigger forks in the road. Stay or go, in or out, do or don't. No doubt, they're all valuable. But if life was solely about these decisions, we'd have massive blinders on to the more common, frequent, and in some cases impactful decisions.

The daily decision of how you show up (mindset, energy, attitude, effort) can be the biggest choice. It's the gap between Winning Monday and getting crushed by Monday. You choose how to show up and enter each day.

When you walk in a room, you either warm it up or you cool it off. *Are you aware of your own temperature? Always.*

Choosing to be the warm light instead of the cold storm can transform your relationships.

Choosing a life of design versus a life of default is a massive separator.

Are you in the game, or on the sidelines?

The choice is always yours.

Practice makes permanent. The reason there are dozens of Decision Drills in this book is for mastery to form. Mastery of making better decisions faster requires reps. Repetition breeds consistency, habits, positive behavior change, and all these elements require a better decision faster to step into this new lifestyle.

You have a choice on the career, relationships, and life you lead. In order to show up at your best, you must deeply know who you are. The Decision Drills in *Better Decisions Faster* challenged you to think, feel, reflect, write, and question what you thought to be true, encouraged you to grow, and, ideally, become the best version of yourself, one decision at a time. Each drill had questions. Answering each question is a decision in and of itself. These Decision Drills are required to make better decisions faster the rest of your life.

In case you missed any or want to revisit, all Decision Drills are here. Just scan the QR code below and let's make some decisions.

It starts with decisions. It ends with purpose. Make no mistake, we attack one Monday at a time. We win the day, then the next, then the next. Results rise, and green-light lifestyles and businesses transform. So now the million-dollar question: WHY are we doing this?

It's simple, in my eyes. The hard work, sacrifices, dedication, and commitment are only worth it if there's a giant **GREEN PAYOUT** at the end. But in this case, a payout isn't money, and the pot of gold isn't paid in one lump sum. The pot of gold is purpose, and the deposits are made daily.

Purpose isn't about a North Star; it's a 365 way of life when you feel meaning and drive impact in each day. Moments are happy; joy is everlasting. Success is achieved; significance is fulfilled. Truth be told, the original title of this book—about two years before launch, when it was ideated—was *ON PURPOSE*. It was a book about achieving daily purpose by putting purpose in action and making the playbook accessible to the world.

When I shared the idea, it still felt so distant and overwhelming for many, so I decided to write a book by the people and for the people. I asked myself, what do the most purpose-centered people I know have in common . . . at the most basic and foundational level? They embody **growth, passion, grit, curiosity, passion, authenticity, gratitude, happiness, courage, service, excellence,** and **impact**.

These green lights are the path to purpose. It's yours for the taking.

Don't go at it alone. #WinMonday is your home away from home. While *Better Decisions Faster* arms you with much of the process, context, frameworks, intel, and inspiration to thrive across all areas of life, know that this is simply the starting point. The book is the foundation. Apply it 365 in perpetuity, and it will be a great life. But that is a macro thought.

My head and heart tell me that if you're still reading, you are a lifelong learner and willing to dive in the weeds. You know you will never stop growing, evolving, building, and pursuing your potential. If that's the case, my message is simple: don't go at it alone.

In the company of like-minded and like-hearted people, our #Win-Monday Community, you will enjoy the journey most through camaraderie and connection. Support will be there, in a dark and dreary red, or the messy middle of yellow. There will also be infinite high-fives when you crush your BDFs and earn a green-light life. Your joy, confidence, and fulfillment will skyrocket.

Consider #WinMonday Community your tribe. It's a home where you belong and are seen and valued. #WinMonday Community is a home for a better future.

The next page lays out every way you can get involved, build momentum, and continue your journey.

Then my parting words.

#WINMONDAY COMMUNITY

WELCOME!

It's time to enjoy the fruits of your labor. Reading this book was not a light lift. This is your tribe to continue growing and keep the impact rolling.

Scan the QR code below to access our very own Win Monday Community gifts, gear, podcast, newsletter, and more.

INDIVIDUAL AND TEAM RESOURCES

Whether you're an individual looking for **a 30-day action plan** or an **online course** to further your learning, or an organizational leader looking for a **keynote** or **team training experience**, all can be found at **paulepsteinspeaks.com** or scan the QR code below.

FINAL NOTE

You have everything you need to Win Monday with unshakable confidence, make better decisions faster, and build the green-light business and lifestyle you deserve. Equation intact. Head, heart, and hands fully ignited.

I've got your back, now and forever.

Rather than say goodbye, shall we link up Monday?

You decide.

My gut says I'll see you there—better and faster.

Paul

ACKNOWLEDGMENTS

GRATITUDE IS ONE OF the brightest green lights in the world. Here is my best attempt to shine a light on those who impacted, inspired, contributed to, or supported *Better Decisions Faster* becoming a reality. From the bottom of my heart: THANK YOU.

Mayra, you are my thunder buddy for life. Thank you for supporting my dreams, which have become OUR dreams. You are the best (and fastest) decision ever made!

PJ, to my little leader—we did it buddy. I hope I'm making you proud. You've already inspired many future books to come. Less pages, more pictures . . . got it! :)

Mom, you are the strongest person I know. Thank you for breathing courage and confidence into me when I needed it most.

Dad, RIP. My happiest moments are running to the top of the hill, seeing you over the horizon, and talking . . . like we used to. I miss you SO much. Every life I impact is because of you. THANK YOU.

Naren at Amplify (Publishing), I'm incredibly proud of our work and partnership. I'm even more stoked about the friendship we've built. Thank you for meeting me at the 50 and beyond.

Brandon at Amplify, can't wait to celebrate this one. As project manager, your fingerprints are all over this blueprint. Every detail matters, and your contributions mattered—a lot.

(Writing) Coach Myles, back-to-back books, baby! You take a written idea, sprinkle in your own, and together we create magic (at least in our eyes!). Couldn't do this without you, my friend.

Caitlin at Amplify, you've turned both books into absolute works of art. The compliments I get behind closed doors on the design are special, and I have you to thank for it.

Conner (my CMO) at Good Wolf and SpeakrBrand—everything I do, you make it shine in ways that are unimaginable. You understand me so well that my voice has become OUR voice. Love ya, brotha.

To my entire PurposePoint fam (Davin, Lisa, Steve, Adam, Coryne, Kurt), your support means more than you'll ever know. Let's continue to lead self, lead others, lead impact, and lead from the front.

Casey (brand strategist guru) at Brand Builders Group, if it wasn't for you, *Better Decisions Faster* isn't even the title! Appreciate the coaching and strategy my man—rocket ships ahead.

Rory (Vaden) and the entire Brand Builders Group community, y'all put me through the branding ringer over the past year, and this book is infinitely stronger for it. Signed, a fellow mission-driven messenger.

Connor, Josh, and the entire Impact Eleven Community, thank you for taking my speaking career to the next level. You fuel the stages and impact that follow books like this in ways I didn't know were possible.

Alec at Gotham Artists, thank you for being an early friend and trusted advisor in the speaking business. I wouldn't be where I am without your guidance, support, and straight-shooting NY perspective!

To all my earliest partners and clients that supported me when this was a budding dream with massive purpose and massive potential impact . . . THANK YOU for believing in our future together. It means the world.

ABOUT THE AUTHOR

PAUL EPSTEIN is a former high-level executive for multiple NFL and NBA teams and the bestselling author of *The Power of Playing Offense*. In 2022, he was named one of *SUCCESS* magazine's top thought leaders who get results—alongside Tony Robbins, Brené Brown, Gary Vaynerchuk, and Mel Robbins—and his work has been featured on ESPN, NBC, Fox Business, and in *USA Today*.

In nearly 15 years as a leader in the world of pro sports, Paul helped take NBA teams from the bottom of the league in revenue to the top two, broke every premium sales revenue metric in Super Bowl history while in the NFL's league office, opened a billion-dollar stadium, and founded the San Francisco 49ers Talent Academy, where he was known as the Why Coach.

As an award-winning keynote speaker, Paul's impact continues off-stage, providing leadership development and culture transformation programs for companies and teams including Amazon, Disney, Johnson & Johnson, NASA, the Los Angeles Lakers, and the Dallas Cowboys.

He's also the founder of the Win Monday Community (an elite personal and professional development network) and host of the *Win Monday* podcast, where he interviews high-profile guests who reveal their secrets of confidence and work-life mastery.

Paul lives in L.A. and is a proud USC Trojan and Michigan Wolverine, father of PJ, and husband to Mayra.